"Jerry does it again, with an in-depth understanding of what it takes 'in the real world' coupled with timeless ancient philosophies. He gives us recipes for success ranging from personal relationships to professional strategies. A truly fascinating and insightful guide for life."

—Vig Sherrill, co-president,
Flextronics Semi-Conductor

"As Sun Tzu's foremost student, Michaelson brings home the personal relevance of this ancient wisdom."

—A. J. Vogl, editor, "Across the Board,"
The Conference Board Magazine

"The Michaelsons' *Sun Tzu for Success* is a masterful combination of ancient wisdom translated into practical strategies, tactics, lessons, and disciplines that can enhance personal and business performance and effectiveness."

—Joel E. Terschak, vice-president of finance and CIO,
Central Soya Company

"Wow!!! This book puts it all together:
Excellent translation clarified with unique subheadings.
Personal applications for doing the right things in life.
Business applications for success in your career."

—Carl Glass, senior vice-president of operations,
Varsity Brands, Inc.

"A practical companion for success. Links Sun Tzu's time-honored wisdom to sound fundamentals that can improve your personal life, business, and career."

—Joseph P. Schneider, president and CEO,
LaCrosse Footwear, Inc.

Sun Tzu
FOR SUCCESS

How to Use *The Art of War* to Master Challenges
and Accomplish the Important Goals in Your Life

By Gerald Michaelson WITH Steven Michaelson

Adams Media Corporation
Avon, MA

Published by
Adams Media Corporation
57 Littlefield Street, Avon, MA 02322 U.S.A.
www.adamsmedia.com

ISBN: 1-58062-776-5

Printed in Canada.

J I H G F E D C B A

Library of Congress Cataloging-in-Publication Data
Michaelson, Gerald A.
    Sun Tzu for success / By Gerald Michaelson and Steven Michaelson.
        p.   cm.
    ISBN 1-58062-776-5
    1. Success. 2. Conduct of life. 3. Sunzi, 6th cent. B.C. Sunzi bing fa.
I. Michaelson, Steven. II. Title.
BJ1611.2 .M49 2003
158—dc21   2002014288

This book is available at quantity discounts for bulk purchases.
For information, call 1-800-872-5627.

This book is dedicated with love
to the successful future of
Danny, Katie, Jessica, and Nicholas

Contents

* Subheadings inserted by authors.

*If the sovereign heeds these strategems of mine
and acts upon them,
he will surely win the war,
and I shall stay with him.*

*If the sovereign neither heeds nor acts upon them,
he will certainly suffer defeat,
and I shall leave.*

—Sun Tzu

Introduction

Sun Tzu's advice for success earns well-deserved recognition because:

The Art of War is the world's first self-help book.

Originally inscribed on bamboo strips about 500 B.C., *The Art of War* is the oldest book ever written. This advice for emperors and generals has the strength of simple timeless wisdom that can be applied to your success.

The simple truths from Sun Tzu underlie much of Eastern strategic thought. Understanding both Eastern and Western strategies can help you be more successful. While Western thought focuses on strategies that engage the opponent, Eastern thought stresses strategies that win before the battle—that is, "winning without fighting."

It has been wisely said that a writer can only exist in the context of the times in which he lives. So it is with Sun Tzu. His writing revolves around the most crucial "art" of his day: the art of war. His thoughts speak volumes about core values, creative ideas, and sound strategies for success.

Personal success arises from who you really are. This self reality transcends the events in our life. It transcends good times and hard times. Who you are transcends the phases of growing up and growing older. Your own reality is difficult to disguise over the short term, and impossible to fake over the long term. The real self is what Sun Tzu recognized as the basis of a good commander. What is inside counts in Sun Tzu's time and ours.

To get where you want to be, you need to know where you are and where you are going. Acquiring this self knowledge about today and tomorrow can be one of the hardest challenges we face. What do we truly want to be and achieve? Only then can we plan our course of action and determine whether we are willing to make the sacrifices required to get to our destination.

It is in the search for understanding how to apply Sun Tzu's wisdom that we find the keys to applying personal strategies. We hope this synthesis of Sun Tzu's 2,500-year-old simple advice may help you reach sound decisions. Our commentary can only underscore the basic principles of Sun Tzu.

We do not suggest taking Sun Tzu's words too literally. His wisdom is simply a thought generator.

In Book One, we present the entire text of *The Art of War* with our subheadings inserted so you can more easily find salient points.

In Book Two, we extract key concepts and discuss how they can be applied to practical strategies for your success.

Comprehensive research of all the English language translations of *The Art of War* has helped us to be faithful to our mission:

1. To coalesce the wisdom from the best translations of Sun Tzu's ancient self-help text.
2. To convert this wisdom into contemporary practical strategies for success in everyday life.

Your success in applying this ancient wisdom is our success. Our every wish is for your continued success.

Gerald A. Michaelson
Steven W. Michaelson

The Lesson of the Concubines

The following story is considered to be of dubious authenticity and not part of the thirteen chapters. Some translators include it within their books, others ignore its existence. All narratives are quite similar. You may find interesting lessons in the following version.

Sun Tzu's book, *The Art of War*, earned him an audience with the King of Wu, who said, "I have thoroughly read your thirteen chapters. May I submit your theory of managing soldiers to a small test?"

Sun Tzu replied, "Sir, you may."

The King of Wu asked, "Can the test be applied to women?"

Sun Tzu replied that it could, so arrangements were made to bring 180 beautiful women from the palace. Sun Tzu divided them into two companies with one of the King's favorite concubines at the head of each. He then made all of them take spears in their hands and spoke to them: "I presume you know the difference between front and back, right hand, and left hand?"

The women replied, "Yes."

Sun Tzu continued, "When to the sound of drums I order 'eyes front,' look straight ahead. When I order 'left turn,' face toward your left hand. When I order 'right turn,' face toward your right hand. When I order 'about turn,' face around to the back."

After the words of command had been explained, the women agreed they understood. He gave them spears so he could begin the drill. To the sound of drums, Sun Tzu ordered 'right turn.' In response, the women burst out in laughter.

With great patience, Sun Tzu said, "If the instructions and words of command are not clear and distinct, if orders are not thoroughly understood, then the general is to blame." He then repeated the explanations several times. This time he ordered the drums to signal 'left turn,' and again the women burst into laughter.

Then Sun Tzu said, "If the instructions and words of command are not clear and distinct, if orders are not thoroughly understood, the general is to blame. But if commands are clear and the soldiers disobey, then it is the fault of the officers." He immediately ordered the women who were at the head of the two companies to be beheaded.

Of course, the King was watching from a raised pavilion, and when he saw that his two favorite concubines were about to be executed, he was alarmed and swiftly sent down a message: "We are now quite satisfied as to the general's ability to manage troops. Without these concubines, my food and drink will not taste good. It is the King's wish that they not be beheaded."

Sun Tzu replied, "Having received the sovereign's commission to take charge and direct these troops, there are certain orders I cannot accept." He immediately had the two concubines beheaded as an example and appointed the two next in line as the new leaders.

Now the drums were sounded and the drill began. The women performed all the maneuvers exactly as commanded, turning to the right or left, marching ahead, turning around, kneeling, or rising. They drilled perfectly in precision and did not utter a single sound.

Sun Tzu sent a messenger to the King of Wu saying, "Your Majesty, the soldiers are now correctly drilled and perfectly disciplined. They are ready for your inspection. Put them to any use you desire. As sovereign, you may choose to require them to go through fire and water and they will not disobey."

The King responded, "Our commander should cease the drill and return to his camp. We do not wish to come down and inspect the troops."

With great calm, Sun Tzu said, "This king is only fond of words and cannot carry them into deeds."

Commentary following this story indicates that the King relented, recognizing Sun Tzu's ability, and appointed him a general; and Sun Tzu won many battles. In contrast, some historians believe Sun Tzu simply served as a civilian strategist, and others deny his existence, claiming he was actually someone else.

The moral of the story could be a lesson on training, discipline, command structure, role playing, or perhaps job interviews. The thoughtful reader may use his or her imagination to determine applicable lessons.

Book One
The Art of War
Sun Tzu

The Complete Text*

*Subheadings inserted by authors.

Preface to Book One

Life on earth is sprinkled with periods of Chinese world leadership. Ancient Chinese minds developed the most advanced technology, the most scientific mindset, the most successful battle strategies, and the world's oldest books.

In this setting of relative prosperity filled with scientific and cultural advancement, thought and resources were devoted to defending your state—or taking your neighbor's. A leading commentary of that time is Sun Tzu's *The Art of War.*

Sun Tzu was neither a general nor a political leader. In today's context, he was more of an advisor, an ad hoc Department of War. In effect, he was a consultant to a variety of warlords and emperors.

His lessons are simple, memorable, and, we think, valuable even today.

A recent translation of *The Art of War* secured while speaking on Sun Tzu in China is presented in its entirety. In Book One that follows, the text is punctuated with subheadings the authors have inserted. Some paragraphs have been relocated. This is done to clarify the content and aid in browsing the original text.

You may choose to scan the translation in Book One and more thoroughly review key concepts drawn from the text discussed in Book Two.

Chapter One

Laying Plans

Thoroughly Assess Conditions

War is a matter of vital importance to the state; a matter of life and death, the road either to survival or to ruin. Hence, it is imperative that it be thoroughly studied.

Therefore, to make assessment of the outcome of a war, one must compare the various conditions of the antagonistic sides in terms of the five constant factors:

1. moral influence
2. weather
3. terrain
4. commander
5. doctrine

These five constant factors should be familiar to every general. He who masters them wins, he who does not is defeated.

Compare the Seven Attributes

Therefore, to forecast the outcome of a war the attributes of the antagonistic sides should be analyzed by making the following seven comparisons:

Pg 3

MI   1. Which sovereign possesses greater moral influence?

MI   2. Which commander is more capable?

W+T   3. Which side holds more favorable conditions in weather and terrain?

Gm   4. On which side are decrees better implemented?

Com   5. Which side is superior in arms?

Doc   6. On which side are officers and men better trained?

Doc   7. Which side is stricter and more impartial in meting out rewards and punishments?

By means of these seven elements, I can forecast victory or defeat.

If the sovereign heeds these stratagems of mine and acts upon them, he will surely win the war, and I shall, therefore, stay with him. If the sovereign neither heeds nor acts upon them, he will certainly suffer defeat, and I shall leave.

Look for Strategic Turns

Having paid attention to the advantages of my stratagems, the commander must create a helpful situation over and beyond the ordinary rules. By "situation," I mean he should act expediently in accordance with what is advantageous in the field and so meet any exigency.

All warfare is based on deception. Therefore, when able to attack, we must pretend to be unable; when employing our forces, we must seem inactive; when we are near, we must make the enemy believe we are far away; when far away, we must make him believe we are near.

Offer a bait to allure the enemy, when he covets small advantages; strike the enemy when he is in disorder. If he is well prepared with substantial strength, take double precautions against him. If he is powerful in action, evade him. If he is angry, seek to discourage him. If he appears humble, make him arrogant. If his forces have taken a good rest, wear them down. If his forces are united, divide them.

Launch the attack where he is unprepared; take action when it is unexpected.

These are the keys to victory for a strategist. However, it is impossible to formulate them in detail beforehand.

Now, the commander who gets many scores during the calculations in the temple before the war will have more likelihood of winning. The commander who gets few scores during the calculations in the temple before the war will have less chance of success. With many scores, one can win; with few scores, one cannot. How much less chance of victory has one who gets no scores at all! By examining the situation through these aspects, I can foresee who is likely to win or lose.

Chapter Two

Waging War

Marshal Adequate Resources

Generally, operations of war involve one thousand swift chariots, one thousand heavy chariots and one hundred thousand mailed troops with the transportation of provisions for them over a thousand *li*. Thus, the expenditure at home and in the field, the stipends for the entertainment of state guests and diplomatic envoys, the cost of materials such as glue and lacquer, and the expense for care and maintenance of chariots and armor, will amount to one thousand pieces of gold a day. An army of one hundred thousand men can be raised only when this money is in hand.

Make Time Your Ally

In directing such an enormous army, a speedy victory is the main object.

If the war is long delayed, the men's weapons will be blunted and their ardor will be dampened. If the army attacks cities, their strength will be exhausted. Again, if the army engages in protracted campaigns, the resources of the state will not suffice. Now, when your weapons are blunted, your ardor dampened, your strength exhausted, and your treasure spent, neighboring rulers will take advantage of your distress to act. In this case, no man, however wise, is able to avert the disastrous consequences that ensue.

Thus, while we have heard of stupid haste in war, we have not yet seen a clever operation that was prolonged. There has never been a case in which a prolonged war has benefited a country. Therefore, only those who understand the dangers inherent in employing troops know how to conduct war in the most profitable way.

Everyone Must Profit from Victories

Those adept in employing troops do not require a second levy of conscripts or more than two provisionings. They carry military supplies from the homeland and make up for their provisions relying on the enemy. Thus, the army will be always plentifully provided.

When a country is impoverished by military operations, it is because an army far from its homeland needs a distant transportation. Being forced to carry supplies for great distances renders the people destitute. On the other hand, the local price of commodities normally rises high in the area near the military camps. The rising prices cause financial resources to be drained away. When the resources are exhausted, the peasantry will be afflicted with urgent exactions. With this depletion of strength and exhaustion of wealth, every household in the homeland is left empty. Seven-tenths of the people's income is dissipated and six-tenths of the government's revenue is paid for broken-down chariots, worn-out horses, armor and helmets, arrows and crossbows, halberds and bucklers, spears and body shields, draught oxen and heavy wagons.

Hence, a wise general is sure of getting provisions from the enemy countries. One *zhong* of grains obtained from the local area is equal to twenty *zhong* shipped from the home country; one *dan* of fodder in the conquered area is equal to twenty *dan* from the domestic store.

Now in order to kill the enemy, our men must be roused to anger; to gain enemy's property, our men must be rewarded with war trophies. Accordingly, in chariot battle, when more than ten chariots have been captured, those who took the enemy chariot first should be rewarded. Then, the enemy's flags and banners should be replaced with ours; the captured chariots mixed with ours and mounted by our men. The prisoners of war should be kindly treated and kept. This is called 'becoming stronger in the course of defeating the enemy."

Know Your Craft

Hence, what is valued in war is a quick victory, not prolonged operations. And, therefore, the general who understands war is the controller of his people's fate and the guarantor of the security of the nation.

Chapter Three

Attack by Strategem

Win Without Fighting

Generally, in war the best thing of all is to take the enemy's state whole and intact; to ruin it is inferior to this. To capture the enemy's entire army is better than to destroy it; to take intact a battalion, a company, or a five-man squad is better than to destroy them. Hence, to win one hundred victories in one hundred battles is not the acme of skill. To subdue the enemy without fighting is the supreme excellence.

Thus, the best policy in war is to attack the enemy's strategy.
The second best way is to disrupt his alliances through diplomatic means.
The next best method is to attack his army in the field.
The worst policy is to attack walled cities. Attacking cities is the last resort when there is no alternative.

It takes at least three months to make mantlets and shielded vehicles ready and prepare necessary arms and equipments. It takes at least another three months to pile up earthen mounds against the walls. The general unable to control his impatience will order his troops to swarm up the wall like ants with the result that one third of them are slain, while the cities remain untaken. Such is the calamity of attacking walled cities.

Therefore, those skilled in war subdue the enemy's army without fighting. They capture the enemy's cities without assaulting them and overthrow his state without protracted operations.

Their aim must be to take all under heaven intact through strategic superiority. Thus, their troops are not worn out and their triumph will be complete. This is the art of attacking by strategem.

Attain Strategic Superiority

Consequently, the art of using troops is this:

When ten to the enemy's one, surround him.
When five times his strength, attack him.
If double his strength, engage him.
If equally matched, be capable of dividing him.
If less in number, be capable of defending yourself.
And, if in all respects unfavorable, be capable of eluding him.
Hence, a weak force will eventually fall captive to a strong one
    if it simply holds ground and conducts a desperate defense.

Beware of "High-Level Dumb"

Now, the general is the bulwark of the state:

If the bulwark is complete at all points, the state will surely
    be strong.
If the bulwark is defective, the state will certainly be weak.

Now, there are three ways in which a sovereign can bring misfortune upon his army:

1. By ordering an advance while ignorant of the fact that the army cannot go forward, or by ordering a retreat while ignorant of the fact that the army cannot fall back. This is described as "hobbling the army."

2. By interfering with the army's administration without knowledge of the internal affairs of the army. This causes officers and soldiers to be perplexed.

3. By interfering with direction of fighting, while ignorant of the military principle of adaptation to circumstances. This sows doubts and misgivings in the minds of his officers and soldiers.

If the army is confused and suspicious, neighboring rulers will take advantage of this and cause trouble. This is simply bringing anarchy into the army and flinging victory away.

Seek Circumstances Which Assure Victory

Thus, there are five points in which victory may be predicted:

1. He who knows when to fight and when not to fight will win.
2. He who understands how to handle both superior and inferior forces will win.
3. He whose ranks are united in purpose will win.
4. He who is well prepared and lies in wait for an enemy who is not well prepared will win.
5. He whose generals are able and not interfered with by the sovereign will win.

It is in these five points that the way to victory is known. Therefore, I say:

Know the enemy and know yourself, and you can fight a hundred battles with no danger of defeat.

When you are ignorant of the enemy but know yourself, your chances of winning and losing are equal.

If ignorant both of your enemy and of yourself, you are sure to be defeated in every battle.

Chapter Four

Disposition of Military Strength

Be Invincible

The skillful warriors in ancient times first made themselves invincible and then awaited the enemy's moment of vulnerability. Invincibility depends on oneself, but the enemy's vulnerability on himself. It follows that those skilled in war can make themselves invincible but cannot cause an enemy to be certainly vulnerable. Therefore, it can be said that, one may know how to achieve victory, but cannot necessarily do so.

Invincibility lies in the defense, the possibility of victory in the attack. Defend yourself when the enemy's strength is abundant, and attack the enemy when it is inadequate.

Those who are skilled in defense hide themselves as under the most secret recesses of earth. Those skilled in attack flash forth as from above the topmost heights of heaven. Thus, they are capable both of protecting themselves and of gaining a complete victory.

Win Without Fighting

To foresee a victory no better than ordinary people's foresight is not the acme of excellence. Neither is it the acme of excellence if you win a victory through fierce fighting and the whole empire says, 'Well done!' Hence, by analogy, to lift an autumn hair [hare] does not signify great strength; to see the sun and moon does not signify good sight; to hear the thunderclap does not signify acute hearing.

In ancient times, those called skilled in war conquered an enemy easily conquered. Consequently, a master of war wins victories without showing his brilliant military success, and without gaining the reputation for wisdom or the merit for valor. He wins his victories without making mistakes. Making no mistakes is what establishes the certainty of victory, for it means that he conquers an enemy already defeated.

Accordingly, a wise commander always ensures that his forces are put in an invincible position, and at the same time will be sure to miss no opportunity to defeat the enemy. It follows that a triumphant army will not fight with the enemy until the victory is assured; while an army destined to defeat will always fight with the opponent first, in the hope that it may win by sheer good luck. The commander adept in war enhances the moral influence and adheres to the laws and regulations. Thus, it is in his power to control success.

Use Information to Focus Resources

Now, the elements of the art of war are first, the measurement of space; second, the estimation of quantities; third, the calculation of figures; fourth, comparisons of strength, and fifth, chances of victory.

Measurements of space are derived from the ground. Quantities derive from measurement, figures from quantities, comparisons from figures, and victory from comparisons.

Therefore, a victorious army is as one *yi* balanced against a grain, and a defeated army is as a grain balanced against one *yi*.

An army superior in strength takes action like the bursting of pent-up waters into a chasm of a thousand fathoms deep. This is what the disposition of military strength means in the actions of war.

Chapter Five

Use of Energy

Build a Sound Organization Structure

Generally, management of a large force is the same in principle as the management of a few men: it is a matter of organization. And to direct a large army to fight is the same as to direct a small one: it is a matter of command signs and signals.

Employ Extraordinary Force

That the whole army can sustain the enemy's all-out attack without suffering defeat is due to operations of extraordinary and normal forces. Troops thrown against the enemy as a grindstone against eggs is an example of the strong beating the weak.

Generally, in battle, use the normal force to engage and use the extraordinary to win. Now, to a commander adept at the use of extra-ordinary forces, his resources are as infinite as the heaven and earth, as inexhaustible as the flow of the running rivers. They end and begin again like the motions of the sun and moon. They die away and then are reborn like the changing of the four seasons.

In battle, there are not more than two kinds of postures—opera-tion of the extraordinary force and operation of the normal force, but their combinations give rise to an endless series of maneuvers. For these two forces are mutually reproductive. It is like moving in circle, never coming to an end. Who can exhaust the possibilities of their combinations?

Coordinate Momentum and Timing

When torrential water tosses boulders, it is because of its momentum; when the strike of a hawk breaks the body of its prey, it is because of timing. Thus, in battle, a good commander creates a posture releasing an irresistible and overwhelming momentum, and his attack is precisely timed in a quick tempo. The energy is similar to a fully drawn crossbow; the timing, the release of the trigger.

Amid turmoil and tumult of battle, there may be seeming disorder and yet no real disorder in one's own troops. In the midst of confusion and chaos, your troops appear to be milling about in circles, yet it is proof against defeat.

Apparent disorder is born of order; apparent cowardice, of courage; apparent weakness, of strength. Order or disorder depends on organization and direction; courage or cowardice on postures; strength or weakness on dispositions.

Thus, one who is adept at keeping the enemy on the move maintains deceitful appearances, according to which the enemy will act. He lures with something that the enemy is certain to take. By so doing he keeps the enemy on the move and then waits for the right moment to make a sudden ambush with picked troops.

Therefore, a skilled commander sets great store by using the situation to the best advantage, and does not make excessive demands on his subordinates. Hence he is able to select the right men and exploits the situation. He who takes advantage of the situation uses his men in fighting as rolling logs or rocks. It is the nature of logs and rocks to stay stationary on the flat ground, and to roll forward on a slope. If four-cornered, they stop; if round-shaped, they roll. Thus, the energy of troops skillfully commanded is just like the momentum of round rocks quickly tumbling down from a mountain thousands of feet in height. This is what 'use of energy' means.

Chapter Six

Weakness and Strength

Take the Initiative

Generally, he who occupies the field of battle first and awaits his enemy is at ease; he who arrives later and joins battle in haste is weary. And, therefore, one skilled in war brings the enemy to the field of battle and is not brought there by him.

One able to make the enemy come of his own accord does so by offering him some advantage. And one able to stop him from coming does so by inflicting damage on him.

Plan Surprise

Thus, when the enemy is at ease, he is able to tire him; when well fed, to starve him; when at rest, to make him move. All these can be done because you appear at points which the enemy must hasten to defend.

That you may march a thousand *li* without tiring yourself is because you travel where there is no enemy.

That you are certain to take what you attack is because you attack a place the enemy does not or cannot protect.

That you are certain of success in holding what you defend is because you defend a place the enemy must hasten to attack.

Therefore, against those skillful in attack, the enemy does not know where to defend, and against the experts in defense, the enemy does not know where to attack.

How subtle and insubstantial that the expert leaves no trace. How divinely mysterious that he is inaudible. Thus, he is master of his enemy's fate.

His offensive will be irresistible if he plunges into the enemy's weak points; he cannot be overtaken when he withdraws if he moves swiftly. Hence, if we wish to fight, the enemy will be compelled to an engagement even though he is safe behind high ramparts and deep ditches. This is because we attack a position he must relieve.

If we do not wish to fight, we can prevent him from engaging us even though the lines of our encampment be merely traced out on the ground. This is because we divert him from going where he wishes.

Gain Relative Superiority

Accordingly, by exposing the enemy's dispositions and remaining invisible ourselves, we can keep our forces concentrated, while the enemy's must be divided. We can form a single united body at one place, while the enemy must scatter his forces at ten places. Thus, it is ten to one when we attack him at one place, which means we are numerically superior. And if we are able to use many to strike few at the selected place, those we deal with will be in dire straits.

The spot where we intend to fight must not be made known. In this way, the enemy must take precautions at many places against the attack. The more places he must guard, the fewer his troops we shall have to face at any given point.

For if he prepares to the front his rear will be weak; and if to the rear, his front will be fragile. If he strengthens his left, his right will be vulnerable; and if his right gets strengthened, there will be few troops on his left. If he sends reinforcements everywhere, he will be weak everywhere.

Numerical weakness comes from having to prepare against possible attacks; numerical strength from compelling the enemy to make these preparations against us.

Practice Good Intelligence

Therefore, if one knows the place and time of the coming battle, his troops can march a thousand *li* and fight on the field. But if one knows neither the spot nor the time, then one cannot manage to have the left wing help the right wing or the right wing help the left; the forces in the front will be unable to support the rear, and the rear will be unable to reinforce the front. How much more so if the furthest portions of the troop deployments extend tens of *li* in breadth, and even the nearest troops are separated by several *li*!

Although I estimate the troops of Yue as many, of what benefit is this superiority in terms of victory?

Thus, I say that victory can be achieved. For even if the enemy is numerically stronger, we can prevent him from fighting.

Therefore, analyze the enemy's battle plan, so as to have a clear understanding of its strong and weak points. Agitate the enemy so as to ascertain his pattern of movement. Lure him in the open so as to find out his vulnerable spots in disposition. Probe him and learn where his strength is abundant and where deficient.

Now, the ultimate in disposing one's troops is to conceal them without ascertainable shape. In this way, the most penetrating spies cannot pry nor can the wise lay plans against you.

Be Flexible

Even though we show people the victory gained by using flexible tactics in conformity to the changing situations, they do not comprehend this. People all know the tactics by which we achieved victory, but they do not know how the tactics were applied in the situation to defeat the enemy. Hence no one victory is gained in the same manner as another.

The tactics change in an infinite variety of ways to suit changes in the circumstances.

Now, the laws of military operations are like water. The tendency of water is to flow from heights to lowlands. The law of successful operations is to avoid the enemy's strength and strike his weakness. Water changes its course in accordance with the contours of the land. The soldier works out his victory in accordance with the situation of the enemy.

Hence, there are neither fixed postures nor constant tactics in warfare. He who can modify his tactics in accordance with the enemy situation and thereby succeeds in winning may be said to be divine. Of the five elements, none is ever predominant; of the four seasons, none lasts forever; of the days, some are longer and others shorter, and of the moon, it sometimes waxes and sometimes wanes.

Chapter Seven

Maneuvering

Maneuver to Gain the Advantage

Normally, in war, the general receives his commands from the sovereign. During the process from assembling the troops and mobilizing the people to deploying the army ready for battle, nothing is more difficult than the art of maneuvering for seizing favorable positions beforehand. What is difficult about it is to make the devious route the most direct and to turn disadvantage to advantage. Thus, forcing the enemy to deviate and slow down his march by luring him with a bait, you may set out after he does and arrive at the battlefield before him. One able to do this shows the knowledge of artifice of deviation.

Thus, both advantage and danger are inherent in maneuvering for an advantageous position. One who sets the entire army in motion with impedimenta to pursue an advantageous position will be too slow to attain it. If he abandons the camp and all the impedimenta to contend for advantage, the baggage and stores will be lost.

It follows that when the army rolls up the armor and sets out speedily, stopping neither day nor night and marching at double speed for a hundred *li* to wrest an advantage, the commander of three divisions will be captured. The vigorous troops will arrive first and the feeble will straggle along behind, so that if this method is used, only one-tenth of the army will arrive. In a forced march of fifty *li*, the commander of the first and van division will fall, and using this method but half of the army will arrive. In a forced march of thirty *li*, but two-thirds will arrive. Hence, the army will be lost without baggage train; and it cannot survive without provisions, nor can it last long without sources of supplies.

Deceive Your Opponent

One who is not acquainted with the designs of his neighbors should not enter into alliances with them. Those who do not know the conditions of mountains and forests, hazardous defiles, and marshes and swamps cannot conduct the march of an army. Those who do not use local guides are unable to obtain the advantages of the ground.

Now, war is based on deception. Move when it is advantageous and change tactics by dispersal and concentration of your troops. When campaigning, be swift as the wind; in leisurely march, be majestic as the forest; in raiding and plundering, be fierce as fire; in standing, be firm as the mountains. When hiding, be as unfathomable as things behind the clouds; when moving, fall like a thunderclap. When you plunder the countryside, divide your forces. When you conquer territory, defend strategic points.

Weigh the situation before you move. He who knows the artifice of deviation will be victorious. Such is the art of maneuvering.

Practice the Art of Good Management

The Book of Army Management says: "As the voice cannot be heard in battle, gongs and drums are used. As troops cannot see each other clearly in battle, flags and banners are used." Hence, in night fighting, usually use drums and gongs; in day fighting, banners and flags. Now, these instruments are used to unify the action of the troops. When the troops can be thus united, the brave cannot advance alone, nor can the cowardly retreat. This is the art of directing large masses of troops.

A whole army may be robbed of its spirit, and its commander deprived of his presence of mind. Now, at the beginning of a campaign, the spirit of soldiers is keen; after a certain period of time, it declines; and in the later stage, it may be dwindled to nought. A clever commander, therefore, avoids the enemy when his spirit is keen and attacks him when it is lost. This is the art of attaching importance to moods. In good order, he awaits a disorderly enemy; in serenity, a clamorous one. This is the art of retaining self-possession. Close to the field of battle, he awaits an enemy coming from afar; at rest, he awaits an exhausted enemy; with well-fed troops, he awaits hungry ones. This is the art of husbanding one's strength.

He refrains from intercepting an enemy whose banners are in perfect order, and desists from attacking an army whose formations are in an impressive array. This is the art of assessing circumstances.

Now, the art of employing troops is that when the enemy occupies high ground, do not confront him uphill, and when his back is resting on hills, do not make a frontal attack. When he pretends to flee, do not pursue. Do not attack soldiers whose temper is keen. Do not swallow a bait offered by the enemy. Do not thwart an enemy who is returning homewards. When you surround an army, leave an outlet free. Do not press a desperate enemy too hard. Such is the method of using troops.

Chapter Eight

Variation of Tactics

Tactics Vary with the Situation

Generally, in war, the general receives his commands from the sovereign, assembles troops, and mobilizes the people. When on grounds hard of access, do not encamp. On grounds intersected with highways, join hands with your allies. Do not linger on critical ground. In encircled ground, resort to strategem. In desperate ground, fight a last-ditch battle.

There are some roads which must not be followed, some troops which must not be attacked, some cities which must not be assaulted, some ground which must not be contested, and some commands of the sovereign which must not be obeyed.

Hence, the general who thoroughly understands the advantages that accompany variation of tactics knows how to employ troops.

The general who does not is unable to use the terrain to his advantage even though he is well acquainted with it. In employing the troops for attack, the general who does not understand the variation of tactics will be unable to use them effectively, even if he is familiar with the Five Advantages.

Carefully Consider Advantages and Disadvantages

And for this reason, a wise general in his deliberations must consider both favorable and unfavorable factors. By taking into account the favorable factors, he makes his plan feasible; by taking into account the unfavorable, he may avoid possible disasters.

What can subdue the hostile neighboring rulers is to hit what hurts them most; what can keep them constantly occupied is to make trouble for them; and what can make them rush about is to offer them ostensible allurements.

It is a doctrine of war that we must not rely on the likelihood of the enemy not coming, but on our own readiness to meet him; not on the chance of his not attacking, but on the fact that we have made our position invincible.

Avoid the Faults of Leadership

There are five dangerous faults which may affect a general:

If reckless, he can be killed.
If cowardly, he can be captured.
If quick-tempered, he can be provoked to rage and make a fool of himself.
If he has too delicate a sense of honor, he is liable to fall into a trap because of an insult.
If he is of a compassionate nature, he may get bothered and upset.

These are the five serious faults of a general, ruinous to the conduct of war. The ruin of the army and the death of the general are inevitable results of these five dangerous faults. They must be deeply pondered.

Chapter Nine

On the March

Occupy Strong Natural Positions

Generally, when an army takes up a position and sizes up the enemy situation, it should pay attention to the following:

When crossing the mountains, be sure to stay in the neighborhood of valleys; when encamping, select high ground facing the sunny side; when high ground is occupied by the enemy, do not ascend to attack. So much for taking up a position in mountains.

After crossing a river, you should get far away from it. When an advancing invader crosses a river, do not meet him in midstream. It is advantageous to allow half his force to get across and then strike. If you wish to fight a battle, you should not go to meet the invader near a river which he has to cross. When encamping in the riverine area, take a position on high ground facing the sun. Do not take a position at the lower reaches of the enemy. This relates to positions near a river.

In crossing salt marshes, your sole concern should be to get over them quickly, without any delay. If you encounter the enemy in a salt marsh, you should take position close to grass and water with trees to your rear. This has to do with taking up a position in salt marshes.

On level ground, take up an accessible position and deploy your main flanks on high grounds with front lower than the back. This is how to take up a position on level ground. These are principles for encamping in the four situations named. By employing them, the Yellow Emperor conquered his four neighboring sovereigns.

Always Seek the High Ground

Generally, in battle and maneuvering, all armies prefer high ground to low, and sunny places to shady. If an army encamps close to water and grass with adequate supplies, it will be free from countless diseases and this will spell victory. When you come to hills, dikes, or embankments, occupy the sunny side, with your main flank at the back. All these methods are advantageous to the army and can exploit the possibilities the ground offers.

When heavy rain falls in the upper reaches of a river and foaming water descends, do not ford and wait until it subsides. When encountering "Precipitous Torrents," "Heavenly Wells," "Heavenly Prison," 'Heavenly Net," "Heavenly Trap," and "Heavenly Cracks," you must march speedily away from them. Do not approach them. While we keep a distance from them, we should draw the enemy toward them. We face them and cause the enemy to put his back to them.

If in the neighborhood of your camp there are dangerous defiles or ponds and low-lying ground overgrown with aquatic grass and reeds or forested mountains with dense tangled undergrowth, they must be thoroughly searched, for these are possible places where ambushes are laid and spies are hidden.

Make an Estimate of the Situation

When the enemy is close at hand and remains quiet, he is relying on a favorable position. When he challenges battle from afar, he wishes to lure you to advance; when he is on easy ground, he must be in an advantageous position. When the trees are seen to move, it means the enemy is advancing; when many screens have been placed in the undergrowth, it is for the purpose of deception. The rising of birds in their flight is the sign of an ambuscade. Startled beasts indicate that a sudden attack is forthcoming.

Dust spurting upwards in high, straight columns indicates the approach of chariots. When it hangs low and is widespread, it betokens that infantry is approaching. When it branches out in different directions, it shows that parties have been sent out to collect firewood. A few clouds of dust moving to and fro signify that the army is camping.

When the enemy's envoys speak in humble terms, but the army continues preparations, that means it will advance. When their language is strong and the enemy pretentiously drives forward, these may be signs that he will retreat. When light chariots first go out and take positions on the wings, it is a sign that the enemy is forming for battle. When the enemy is not in dire straits but asks for a truce, he must be plotting. When his troops march speedily and parade in formations, he is expecting to fight a decisive battle on a fixed date. When half his force advances and half retreats, he is attempting to decoy you.

When his troops lean on their weapons, they are famished. When drawers of water drink before carrying it to camp, his troops are suffering from thirst. When the enemy sees an advantage but does not advance to seize it, he is fatigued.

When birds gather above his camp sites, they are unoccupied. When at night the enemy's camp is clamorous, it betokens nervousness. If there is disturbance in the camp, the general's authority is weak.

If the banners and flags are shifted about, sedition is afoot. If the officers are angry, it means that men are weary. When the enemy feeds his horses with grain, kills the beasts of burden for food, and packs up the utensils used for drawing water, he shows no intention to return to his tents and is determined to fight to the death.

When the general speaks in meek and subservient tone to his subordinates, he has lost the support of his men. Too frequent rewards indicate that the general is at the end of his resources; too frequent punishments indicate that he is in dire distress. If the officers at first treat the men violently and later are fearful of them, it shows supreme lack of intelligence.

When envoys are sent with compliments in their mouths, it is a sign that the enemy wishes for a truce.

When the enemy's troops march up angrily and remain facing yours for a long time, neither joining battle nor withdrawing, the situation demands great vigilance and thorough investigation.

In war, numbers alone confer no advantage. If one does not advance by force recklessly, and is able to concentrate his military power through a correct assessment of the enemy situation and enjoys full support of his men, that would suffice. He who lacks foresight and underestimates his enemy will surely be captured by him.

Generate a Fair and Harmonious Relationship

If troops are punished before they have grown attached to you, they will be disobedient. If not obedient, it is difficult to employ them. If troops have become attached to you, but discipline is not enforced, you cannot employ them either. Thus, soldiers must be treated in the first instance with humanity, but kept under control by iron discipline. In this way, the allegiance of soldiers is assured.

If orders are consistently carried out and the troops are strictly supervised, they will be obedient. If orders are never carried out, they will be disobedient. And the smooth implementation of orders reflects harmonious relationship between the commander and his troops.

Chapter Ten

Terrain

Know the Battlefield

Ground may be classified according to its nature as accessible, entangling, temporizing, constricted, precipitous, and distant.

> Ground which both we and the enemy can traverse with equal ease is called accessible. On such ground, he who first takes high sunny positions, and keeps his supply routes unimpeded can fight advantageously.
>
> Ground easy to reach but difficult to exit is called entangling. The nature of this ground is such that if the enemy is unprepared and you sally out, you may defeat him. But, if the enemy is prepared for your coming, and you fail to defeat him, then, return being difficult, disadvantages will ensue.
>
> Ground equally disadvantageous for both the enemy and ourselves to enter is called temporizing. The nature of this ground is such that even though the enemy should offer us an attractive bait, it will be advisable not to go forth but march off. When his force is halfway out because of our maneuvering, we can strike him with advantage.

29

With regard to the constricted ground, if we first occupy it, we must block the narrow passes with strong garrisons and wait for the enemy. Should the enemy first occupy such ground, do not attack him if the pass in his hand is fully garrisoned, but only if it is weakly garrisoned.

With regard to the precipitous ground, if we first occupy it, we must take a position on the sunny heights and await the enemy. If he first occupies such ground, we should march off and not attack him.

When the enemy is situated at a great distance from us, and the terrain where the two armies deploy is similar, it is difficult to provoke battle and unprofitable to engage him.

These are the principles relating to six different types of ground. It is the highest responsibility of the general to inquire into them with the utmost care.

Leaders Must Lead

There are six situations that cause an army to fail. They are: flight, insubordination, fall, collapse, disorganization, and rout. None of these disasters can be attributed to natural and geographical causes, but to the fault of the general.

Terrain conditions being equal, if a force attacks one ten times its size, the result is flight.

When the soldiers are strong and officers weak, the army is insubordinate.

When the officers are valiant and the soldiers ineffective, the army will fall.

When the higher officers are angry and insubordinate, and on encountering the enemy, rush to battle on their own account from a feeling of resentment, and the commander-in-chief is ignorant of their abilities, the result is collapse.

When the general is incompetent and has little authority, when his troops are mismanaged, when the relationship between the officers and men is strained, and when the troop formations are slovenly, the result is disorganization.

When a general unable to estimate the enemy's strength uses a small force to engage a larger one or weak troops to strike the strong, or fails to select shock troops for the van, the result is rout.

When any of these six situations exists, the army is on the road to defeat. It is the highest responsibility of the general that he examine them carefully.

Know the Situation and Your People

Conformation of the ground is of great assistance in the military operations. It is necessary for a wise general to make correct assessments of the enemy's situation to create conditions leading to victory and to calculate distances and the degree of difficulty of the terrain. He who knows these things and applies them to fighting will definitely win. He who knows them not, and is, therefore, unable to apply them, will definitely lose.

Hence, if, in the light of the prevailing situation, fighting is sure to result in victory, then you may decide to fight even though the sovereign has issued an order not to engage.

If fighting does not stand a good chance of victory, you need not fight even though the sovereign has issued an order to engage.

Hence, the general who advances without coveting fame and retreats without fearing disgrace, whose only purpose is to protect his people and promote the best interests of his sovereign, is the precious jewel of the state.

If a general regards his men as infants, then they will march with him into the deepest valleys. He treats them as his own beloved sons and they will stand by him unto death. If, however, a general is indulgent towards his men but cannot employ them, cherishes them but cannot command them or inflict punishment on them when they violate the regulations, then they may be compared to spoiled children, and are useless for any practical purpose.

Know Yourself and Your Opponent

If we know that our troops are capable of striking the enemy, but do not know that he is invulnerable to attack, our chance of victory is but half.

If we know that the enemy is vulnerable to attack but do not know that our troops are incapable of striking him, our chance of victory is again but half.

If we know that the enemy can be attacked and that our troops are capable of attacking him, but do not realize that the conformation of the ground makes fighting impracticable, our chance of victory is once again but half.

Therefore, those experienced in war moves are never bewildered; when they act, they are never at a loss. Thus, the saying: Know the enemy and know yourself, and your victory will never be endangered; know the weather and know the ground, and your victory will then be complete.

Chapter Eleven

The Nine Varieties of Ground

Choose the Battleground

In respect to the employment of troops, ground may be classified as dispersive, frontier, key, open, focal, serious, difficult, encircled, and desperate.

When a chieftain is fighting in his own territory, he is in dispersive ground. When he has penetrated into hostile territory, but to no great distance, he is in frontier ground. Ground equally advantageous for us and the enemy to occupy is key ground. Ground equally accessible to both sides is open. Ground contiguous to three other states is focal. He who first gets control of it will gain the support of the majority of neighboring states. When an army has penetrated deep into hostile territory, leaving far behind many enemy cities and towns, it is in serious ground. Mountain forests, rugged steeps, marshes, fens and all that is hard to traverse fall into the category of difficult ground. Ground to which access is constricted and from which we can only retire by tortuous paths so that a small number of the enemy would suffice to crush a large body of our men is encircled ground. Ground on which the army can avoid annihilation only through a desperate fight without delay is called a desperate one.

And, therefore, do not fight in dispersive ground; do not stop in the frontier borderlands.

Do not attack an enemy who has occupied key ground; in open ground, do not allow your communication to be blocked.

In focal ground, form alliances with neighboring states; in serious ground, gather in plunder.

In difficult ground, press on; in encircled ground, resort to stratagems; and in desperate ground, fight courageously.

Shape Your Opponent's Strategy

In ancient times, those described as skilled in war knew how to make it impossible for the enemy to unite his van and his rear, for his large and small divisions to cooperate, for his officers and men to support each other, and for the higher and lower levels of the enemy to establish contact with each other.

When the enemy's forces were dispersed, they prevented him from assembling them; even when assembled, they managed to throw his forces into disorder. They moved forward when it was advantageous to do so; when not advantageous, they halted.

Should one ask: "How do I cope with a well-ordered enemy host about to attack me?" I reply: "seize something he cherishes and he will conform to your desires."

Speed is the essence of war. Take advantage of the enemy's unpreparedness, make your way by unexpected routes, and attack him where he has taken no precautions.

Victory Is the Only Option

The general principles applicable to an invading force are that the deeper you penetrate into hostile territory, the greater will be the solidarity of your troops, and, thus, the defenders cannot overcome you.

Plunder fertile country to supply your army with plentiful food. Pay attention to the soldiers' well-being and do not fatigue them. Try to keep them in high spirits and conserve their energy. Keep the army moving and devise unfathomable plans.

Throw your soldiers into a position whence there is no escape, and they will choose death over desertion. For if prepared to die, how can the officers and men not exert their uttermost strength to fight? In a desperate situation, they fear nothing; when there is no way out, they stand firm. Deep in a hostile land they are bound together. If there is no help for it, they will fight hard.

Thus, without waiting to be marshaled, the soldiers will be constantly vigilant; without waiting to be asked, they will do your will; without restrictions, they will be faithful; without giving orders, they can be trusted.

Prohibit superstitious practices and do away with rumors. Then nobody will flee even facing death. Our soldiers have no surplus of wealth, but it is not because they disdain riches; they have no expectation of long life, but it is not because they dislike longevity.

On the day the army is ordered out to battle, your soldiers may weep, those sitting up wetting their garments, and those lying down letting the tears run down their cheeks. But throw them into a situation where there is no escape and they will display the immortal courage of Zhuan Zhu and Cao Kuei.

Troops directed by a skillful general are comparable to the Shuai Ran. The Shuai Ran is a snake found in Mount Heng. Strike at its head, and you will be attacked by its tail; strike at its tail, and you will be attacked by its head; strike at its middle, and you will be attacked by both its head and its tail. Should one ask: 'Can troops be made capable of such instantaneous coordination as the Shuai Ran?' I reply: 'They can.' For the men of Wu and the men of Yue are enemies, yet if they are crossing a river in the same boat and are caught by a storm, they will come to each other's assistance just as the left hand helps the right.

Hence, it is not sufficient to rely upon tethering of the horses and the burying of the chariots. The principle of military administration is to achieve a uniform level of courage. The principle of terrain application is to make the best use of both the high- and the low-lying grounds.

Thus, a skillful general conducts his army just as if he were leading a single man, willy-nilly, by the hand.

It is the business of a general to be quiet and thus ensure depth in deliberation; impartial and upright, and, thus, keep a good management.

He should be able to mystify his officers and men by false reports and appearances, and, thus, keep them in total ignorance. He changes his arrangements and alters his plans in order to make others unable to see through his strategies. He shifts his campsites and undertakes marches by devious routes so as to make it impossible for others to anticipate his objective.

He orders his troops for a decisive battle on a fixed date and cuts off their return route, as if he kicks away the ladder behind the soldiers when they have climbed up a height. When he leads his army deep into hostile territory, their momentum is trigger-released in battle. He drives his men now in one direction, then in another, like a shepherd driving a flock of sheep, and no one knows where he is going. To assemble the host of his army and bring it into danger—this may be termed the business of the general.

Learn Winning Ways

The different measures appropriate to the nine varieties of ground and the expediency of advance or withdrawal in accordance with circumstances and the fundamental laws of human nature are matters that must be studied carefully by a general.

Generally, when invading a hostile territory, the deeper the troops penetrate, the more cohesive they will be; penetrating only a short way causes dispersion.

When you leave your own country behind and take your army across neighboring territory, you find yourself on critical ground.

When there are means of communication on all four sides, it
  is focal ground.
When you penetrate deeply into a country, it is serious ground.
When you penetrate but a little way, it is frontier ground.
When you have the enemy's strongholds on your rear, and
  narrow passes in front, it is encircled ground.
When there is no place of refuge at all, it is desperate ground.

Therefore, in dispersive ground, I would unify the determination
of the army. In frontier ground, I would keep my forces closely linked.
In key ground, I would hasten up my rear elements. In open ground, I
would pay close attention to my defense. In focal ground, I would consolidate my alliances. In serious ground, I would ensure a continuous
flow of provisions. In difficult ground, I would press on over the road.
In encircled ground, I would block the points of access and egress. In
desperate ground, I would make it evident that there is no chance of
survival. For it is the nature of soldiers to resist when surrounded, to
fight hard when there is no alternative, and to follow commands
implicitly when they have fallen into danger.

One ignorant of the designs of neighboring states cannot enter into
alliance with them. If ignorant of the conditions of mountains, forests,
dangerous defiles, swamps, and marshes, he cannot conduct the march
of an army. If he fails to make use of native guides, he cannot gain the
advantages of the ground.

An army does not deserve the title of the invincible Army of the
Hegemonic King if its commander is ignorant of even one of these
nine varieties of ground. Now, when such an invincible army attacks
a powerful state, it makes it impossible for the enemy to assemble his
forces. It overawes the enemy and prevents his allies from joining
him. It follows that one does not need to seek alliances with other
neighboring states, nor is there any need to foster the power of other
states, but only to pursue one's own strategic designs to overawe his
enemy. Then one can take the enemy's cities and overthrow the
enemy's state.

Bestow rewards irrespective of customary practice and issue orders irrespective of convention and you can command a whole army as though it were but one man.

Set the troops to their tasks without revealing your designs. When the task is dangerous, do not tell them its advantageous aspect. Throw them into a perilous situation and they will survive; put them in desperate ground and they will live. For when the army is placed in such a situation, it can snatch victory from defeat.

Now, the key to military operations lies in cautiously studying enemy's designs. Concentrate your forces in the main direction against the enemy and from a distance of a thousand *li* you can kill his general. This is called the ability to achieve one's aim in an artful and ingenious manner.

Therefore, on the day the decision is made to launch war, you should close the passes, destroy the official tallies, and stop the passage of all emissaries. Examine the plan closely in the temple council and make final arrangements.

If the enemy leaves a door open, you must rush in. Seize the place the enemy values without making an appointment for battle with him. Be flexible and decide your line of action according to the situation on the enemy side.

At first, then, exhibit the coyness of a maiden until the enemy gives you an opening; afterwards be swift as a running hare, and it will be too late for the enemy to oppose you.

Chapter Twelve

Attack By Fire

Be Disruptive and Intrusive

There are five ways of attacking with fire. The first is to burn soldiers in their camp; the second, to burn provision and stores; the third, to burn baggage-trains; the fourth, to burn arsenals and magazines; and the fifth, to burn the lines of transportation.

To use fire, some medium must be relied upon. Materials for setting fire must always be at hand. There are suitable seasons to attack with fire, and special days for starting a conflagration. The suitable seasons are when the weather is very dry; the special days are those when the moon is in the constellations of the Sieve, the Wall, the Wing or the Cross-bar; for when the moon is in these positions there are likely to be strong winds all day long.

Now, in attacking with fire, one must respond to the five changing situations: When fire breaks out in the enemy's camp, immediately coordinate your action from without. If there is an outbreak of fire, but the enemy's soldiers remain calm, bide your time and do not attack. When the force of the flames has reached its height, follow it up with an attack, if that is practicable; if not, stay where you are. If fires can be raised from outside the enemy's camps, it is not necessary to wait until they are started inside. Attack with fire only when the moment is suitable. If the fire starts from up-wind, do not launch attack from down-wind. When the wind continues blowing during the day, then it is likely to die down at night.

Now, the army must know the five different fire-attack situations and wait for appropriate times.

Those who use fire to assist their attacks can achieve tangible results; those who use inundations can make their attacks more powerful. Water can intercept and isolate an enemy, but cannot deprive him of the supplies or equipment.

Consolidate Your Gains

Now, to win battles and capture lands and cities, but to fail to consolidate these achievements is ominous and may be described as a waste of resources and time. And, therefore, the enlightened rulers must deliberate upon the plans to go to battle, and good generals carefully execute them.

Exercise Restraint

If not in the interests of the state, do not act. If you are not sure of success, do not use troops. If you are not in danger, do not fight a battle.

A sovereign should not launch a war simply out of anger, nor should a general fight a war simply out of resentment. Take action if it is to your advantage; cancel the action if it is not. An angered man can be happy again, just as a resentful one can feel pleased again, but a state that has perished can never revive, nor can a dead man be brought back to life.

Therefore, with regard to the matter of war, the enlightened ruler is prudent, and the good general is full of caution. Thus, the state is kept secure and the army preserved.

Chapter Thirteen

Employment of Secret Agents

Budget Adequate Funds

Generally, when an army of one hundred thousand is raised and dispatched on a distant war, the expenses borne by the people together with the disbursements made by the treasury will amount to a thousand pieces of gold per day. There will be continuous commotion both at home and abroad; people will be involved with convoys and exhausted from performing transportation services, and seven hundred thousand households will be unable to continue their farmwork.

Hostile armies confront each other for years in order to struggle for victory in a decisive battle; yet if one who begrudges the expenditure of one hundred pieces of gold in honors and emoluments remains ignorant of his enemy's situation, he is completely devoid of humanity. Such a man is no leader of the troops; no capable assistant to his sovereign; no master of victory.

Establish an Active Intelligence System

Now, the reason that the enlightened sovereign and the wise general conquer the enemy whenever they move and their achievements surpass those of ordinary men is that they have foreknowledge. This "foreknowledge" cannot be elicited from spirits, nor from gods, nor by analogy with past events, nor by any deductive calculations. It must be obtained from the men who know the enemy situation.

Hence, there are five sorts of spies: native, internal, converted, doomed, and surviving.

When all these five sorts of spies are at work and none knows their method of operation, it would be divinely intricate and constitutes the greatest treasure of a sovereign.

Native spies are those we employ from the enemy's country
    people.
Internal spies are enemy officials whom we employ.
Converted spies are enemy spies whom we employ.
Doomed spies are those of our own spies who are deliberately
    given false information and told to report it.
Surviving spies are those who return from the enemy camp to
    report information.

Hence, of all those in the army close to the commander, none is more intimate than the spies; of all rewards, none more liberal than those given to spies; of all matters, none is more confidential than those relating to spying operations.

He who is not sage cannot use spies. He who is not humane and generous cannot use spies. And he who is not delicate and subtle cannot get the truth out of them. Truly delicate indeed!

There is no place where espionage is not possible. If plans relating to spying operations are prematurely divulged, the spy and all those to whom he spoke of them should be put to death.

Generally, whether it be armies that you wish to strike, cities that you wish to attack, or individuals whom you wish to assassinate, it is necessary to find out the names of the garrison commander, the aides-de-camp, the ushers, gatekeepers, and bodyguards. You must instruct your spies to ascertain these matters in minute detail.

It is essential to seek out enemy spies who have come to conduct espionage against you and bribe them to serve you. Courteously exhort them and give your instructions, then release them back home. Thus, converted spies are recruited and used. It is through the information brought by the converted spies that native and internal spies can be recruited and employed. It is owing to their information, again, that the doomed spies, armed with false information, can be sent to convey it to the enemy. Lastly, it is by their information that the surviving spies can come back and give information as scheduled. The sovereign must have full knowledge of the activities of the five sorts of spies. And to know these depends upon the converted spies. Therefore, it is mandatory that they be treated with the utmost liberality.

In ancient times, the rise of the Shang Dynasty was due to Yi Zhi, who had served under the Xia. Likewise, the rise of the Zhou Dynasty was due to Lu Ya, who had served under the Yin. Therefore, it is only the enlightened sovereign and the wise general who are able to use the most intelligent people as spies and achieve great results. Spying operations are essential in war; upon them the army relies to make its every move.

Translated by Pan Jiabin and Liu Ruixiang
Peoples Republic of China

Book Two
The Art of Success

Preface to Book Two

In Book Two, key excerpts representing major concepts for success are extracted from *The Art of War*. Each is discussed in detail.

The commentary aids in understanding how to apply Sun Tzu's fundamental wisdom. The discussion is organized to take Sun Tzu's advice and apply it to action today.

Section 1. *Personal Characteristics for Success*. This focuses on applying Sun Tzu's wisdom to assessing personal strengths and weaknesses.

Section 2. *Strategies for Success*. Here we explore the Master's advice for finding pathways to success.

Section 3. *Tactics for Success*. Now we move from ancient to modern ideas for taking action successfully.

Section 4. *Success in Competitive Situations*. This discussion stresses how to succeed in everyday battles.

Section 5. *Examples of Personal Success*. Successful people tell how they have applied the Master's strategies.

Section One
Personal Characteristics
for Success

Introduction

Who Are You?

The question "Who are you?" is the foundation for a never-ending journey to success. One can look to Sun Tzu's *The Art of War* for short- and long-term guideposts on this quest. Sun Tzu emphasized knowledge as the pillar of our life plans. In applying his concepts and principles for success, Sun Tzu prescribed specific behaviors that could be learned, practiced, and integrated into daily life.

Sun Tzu's philosophy rests on deep foundations that cannot be fabricated or changed easily. His prescriptions start from questioning and discovering who you are. To achieve the full value from Sun Tzu and his thoughts, you need a solid foundation. This first section is therefore about the personal characteristics that are the foundation for success.

As a moral teacher, Sun Tzu expected the same moral values in his students. Our challenge in today's world is to program consistency into "who we are." From deep within us, we need to avoid "just fake it" and turn on the internal automatic pilot of "just do it" the right way for the right reasons.

Know Yourself

Know the enemy and know yourself,
and you can fight a hundred battles
with no danger of defeat.

If ignorant both of your enemy and yourself,
you are sure to be defeated in every battle.

—Sun Tzu

A famous cartoon possum named Pogo said to his friend Albert the alligator:

We have met the enemy and he is us.

Perhaps he read Sun Tzu.

How many times have you made the observation, "They are their own worst enemy?" It is difficult to perceive ourselves as "the enemy" in any situation. Yet accurate self-perception is the golden key to success.

No one can tell you who you really are; everyone can help in the search. The problem lies not only in your perception, but also in your confidence in your perception. The more accurately you understand your real strengths and weaknesses, the more effective you can be in every endeavor.

Each of us is perceived as three different people:

Who we think we are;

Who others think we are; and

Who we really are.

The most important of these is "who we really are." This search for identity can be the quest of a lifetime.

Identify Your Personality

Our ability to identify ourselves is apparent in the administration of the widely used personality test, the Myers-Briggs Type Indicator. During this process, participants are asked to self-select individual preferences in four categories prior to completing a questionnaire that automatically measures their preferences and personality type. The match is often close between self-selected preferences and preferences measured by the instrument. When the two differ, people are advised that only *they* can know their real preferences.

Among the personality differences identified by Myers-Briggs are thinkers and feelers:

> Thinkers tend to base their decisions on logic. They are interested in analyzing factual data concerning the situation.
> Feelers make their decisions based on personal values and emotions. Feelers are less concerned with objective data and more concerned with how the decision affects people.

Although each of us makes some decisions based on emotion and some decisions based on logic, we do have a tendency to frequently act one way or the other. In general, whatever way we tend to favor in making decisions is the same method we favor in convincing others.

Base your arguments on the decision preference of the person you are trying to convince, not your own. To know their preferences, you must first know your own.

Knowledge of your preferences can be obtained by thinking about the people with whom you associate most comfortably. Often they have the same personality preferences and arrive at decisions in the same manner as you do. Looking at your closest friends can provide a mirror image of yourself.

The more you know about yourself and the reasons for your own preferences and actions, the more you know about others. Self-knowledge breeds a universe of knowledge about human dynamics.

As a young manager, I visited an organization that administered tests, interviewed me, and gave an oral review and written report of my qualifications. At the time I did not believe or understand all of their observations. Over a period of years, I saw my actions mirrored in the written report and developed a greater confidence in my strengths.

A review of this kind has three benefits:

1. You learn about yourself more quickly—eventually, time will reveal your true identity.
2. You achieve a deeper understanding of where your compass should point.
3. You can share the experience with employment interviewers who will be impressed by your efforts to learn more about yourself.

In contemporary management circles this idea of self-analysis is given life in how employers develop their people. Yesterday, the annual performance review was the vehicle for providing self-knowledge in the business world. During the review, your supervisor advised on where you needed to improve and grow. Today, performance is evaluated with 360-degree feedback from peers, subordinates, and bosses who provide information on how you are perceived and what you need to fine-tune in order to achieve objectives.

Head for the Next Level

Here is an overview of ingredients that can start you on the path to applying self-knowledge in your journey to the next level.

- *Determine your values.* At the core of your beliefs, what are the values that drive you? What has driven you to achieve success and what has influenced your failures? What are your priorities? Every decision you make reveals something about yourself. Finding common links is a powerful way to uncover "who you are." Write down your observations.

At age twenty-six, Ben Franklin outlined his own list of personal values.

- *Show commitment.* The core values that make you who you are seldom change. This commitment establishes your identity and determines your future.
- *Accept the help of others.* It is the assistance of others that helps you determine your true identity. Finding out "who you are" is best achieved with the help of someone who can be a sounding board.
- *Think positive.* You have faults that need to be recognized and minimized. Be humble, but not to the extent that humility makes you set your goals too low. Success is achieved by focusing on, and taking advantage of, your inherent strengths. One wins by leading with strength.

An experiment conducted years ago at Hawthorne laboratories is recognized as revealing the beneficial effects of positive psychology. In short, "The Hawthorne Effect" says people who believe good things are happening are motivated to do better. That is, the more strongly you believe things are going well, the more likely you are to be motivated to excel. Conversely, the more you believe things are getting worse, the lower your motivation will be to improve.

Plan Self-Improvement

Everything on earth is either green and growing—or ripe and rotting. As long as you are green and willing to learn new things you are growing. You either get better or you get worse. You grow or decay. It's when you think you have all the answers that you are ripe and rotting.

In his classic book, *How to Win Friends and Influence People,* Dale Carnegie wrote:

> [*Improving yourself*] *is a lot more profitable than trying to improve others.*

Ancient Chinese philosopher, Lao Tzu, reveals an important truth when he states:

> *One who knows others is wise.*
> *One who knows one's self is enlightened.*

At every Winter Olympics we see athletes standing at the top of the hill mentally rehearsing their route to victory—with no spills or misses. These champions are not deluding themselves; they simply believe in what they have practiced and have confidence in their abilities.

Grow Through Relationships

Relationships are one of the most important vehicles for self-growth. Relationships—be they with your boss, your colleagues, your spouse, or your family—are a mirror of your strengths and weaknesses, as well as your values and desires. We all want to be involved with people with similar interests and values. We all want to create relationships that reflect our best qualities back to us.

Honest sharing builds "closeness." When you sincerely express emotion you build intimacy and camaraderie. More importantly, you engage others in your personal development. "Opening up" and sharing personal experiences builds feelings of closeness with others and, in the long run, fosters intimacy with yourself.

Take a sincere interest in others. If you can't be sincere, don't bother. But don't miss the opportunity to "follow your gut" when an opportunity arises and take the time to help. Although you may know many people, you can't know each of their concerns. But when someone needs your help (whether they ask for it or you just "pick up on it"), that is an opportunity.

What makes it challenging is that people generally don't need help at a time of your choosing. Offering help is often inconvenient and gets in the way of other plans. Think about assistance as "caring about one individual at a time." You can't continually care about every person you know. But when the need arises, one person at a time, you can care about that person at that time.

Share values. Some of us easily and comfortably share our values in conversations, interviews, and how we ask questions. Keeping alert can help you identify people with whom you can share a common purpose. These like-minded people will be "attracted" to you and you to them. When you want help reaching a goal, start with a group of people who share your common values and who can become a committed team.

In your quest for personal success you have to make decisions. You won't always make the right ones along the way but strong relationships can help you overcome setbacks en route to your goals.

In Summary

Be who you are.
Be enlightened—know who you are.
Self-knowledge is the foundation of success.

Have Moral Integrity

*The commander adept in war
enhances the moral influence
and adheres to the laws and regulations.*

Thus, it is in his power to control success.
—Sun Tzu

The strength of moral influence is at the heart of Sun Tzu's ability to lead an army. Moral integrity is a characteristic of successful leaders.

Develop a Sense of Moral Integrity

Former Prime Minister of Israel, Benjamin Netanyahu, states the fundamental importance of "moral clarity" in describing key components necessary to winning the war against terrorism: Moral clarity is simply being clear about what is right and what is wrong.

We saw this when American national leaders made America's moral stand clear by declaring there is no excuse for terrorism. It is a "given" in conflict that both sides think "right" is on their side. By being "right," leaders are simply following Sun Tzu's advice on the role of moral influence in getting people in harmony with their objectives.

Netanyahu states the following moral imperatives for victory:

- A military victory cannot be secured until it has been secured as a political victory.

- A political victory cannot be secured until it has been secured with public relations.
- A public relations victory cannot be secured until it has been secured in a sense of justice.

Netanyahu built his argument for Israel's position by starting with a sense of justice. He tells of having dinner one night with the Prime Minister of Spain who questioned him about Israel being on land that at one time belonged to others. The Prime Minister asked Netanyahu, in this historical context how could Israel have a right to exist?

Netanyahu responded, "Why does Spain have a right to exist?" Startled, the Prime Minister of Spain asked him to explain this question. So Netanyahu pointed out that for centuries all of Spain was controlled by the Moors, except for one little piece of land in the North. From that base in the Northern Iberian Peninsula, over a span of decades, Spain succeeded in retaking their country and expelling the Moors.

No one has ever questioned the Spaniards right to their land, because the Spaniards never gave up that right. Netanyahu asked why would it be any different for Israel, which has a clear claim to the land going back to the Old Testament, and is a claim no Jew or Israeli has ever given up?

You may, or may not, agree with Netanyahu's line of reasoning. But, one can only imagine the power that argument had with the Prime Minister of Spain! Obviously, this logic has great moral influence in motivating the people of Israel and those who support the Israeli position in the Holy Land. Note that this argument for the State of Israel is not rooted in power, guns, or pity, but rather in logic that has a moral base.

On the flip side, throughout history, some of the greatest evils have been perpetrated in conjunction with a sense of moral right. Leaders gained support for their actions by justifying a supposedly moral position to their people—often at the expense of integrity.

Harness the Power of Integrity

In our interactions, the word that most clearly sums up moral influence is integrity—defined as adherence to a code. We can have integrity in adherence to a variety of codes—artistic, legal, or moral. In our culture, people who "do not have integrity" generally are viewed as not having adhered to a moral code. Lack of integrity destroys "moral influence."

Integrity is the bedrock of personal reputation. Personal reputation is based on others' perceptions of our behavior. A strong base of integrity gives you the leverage to build your reputation and execute a plan for your personal success. To strengthen your position on an issue, look to the power of moral integrity.

The value of integrity shows up in many different thoughts:

- *Integrity without knowledge is weak and useless. Knowledge without integrity is dangerous and dreadful.*

    —Samuel Johnson

- *A little integrity is better than any career.*

    —Ralph Waldo Emerson

Morality and integrity influence us into "going the extra mile." These same virtues influence relationships in both overt and subtle ways. Often, it's the subtleties of morality and integrity about which we lack understanding. These same subtleties drive so much of our success and interactions in life. Depending on the moral influence present in a relationship, consequences can be either good or bad. When the bad catches up with you, a setback can occur. Here's an example:

Recently, Notre Dame lost a football coach who arguably "fudged" on his integrity. Officials at Notre Dame knew that hiring the head football coach from Georgia Tech was a somewhat controversial call. This head coach had been accused of abusing a football player only a year earlier. The story was that a player had been gang tackled by four other players for missing a blocking assignment. The Notre Dame officials supposedly pushed hard on this point during their interviews with the head coach from Georgia Tech. Eventually, they came away impressed and publicly praising him for his integrity offered him the position at Notre Dame.

Yet, just five days later the new coach was forced to resign over a series of old lies. Not really big lies—he's a football coach after all and his win-loss record is what counts. The new coach claimed to have a Master's degree he clearly had never earned. This "degree" had apparently been on his resume for years. The Notre Dame athletic department responded with the following statement, "We understand these inaccuracies represent a very human failing; nonetheless, they constitute a breach of trust that makes it impossible for us to go forward with our relationship." In resigning, the new coach could only say, "The integrity and credibility of Notre Dame is impeccable, and with that in mind, I will resign my position as head football coach."

The story ended unhappily for everyone. The lie probably did not win the coach the new position but it did cost him the job.

Is this an extreme story? The consequences are extreme but the situation is all too common. When a professional executive-search consultant checked my background and college degrees on my resume, I casually inquired how often someone lies about college degrees on their resume. The consultant replied "In my experience, about 1 in 10!"

In building personal success, the foundation is your personal integrity. Although integrity does not guarantee success, lack of integrity is a prescription for failure. We all know successful people whose integrity is in doubt and will, like the Notre Dame football coach who had to resign, pay a huge price. Building your personal success on a base of integrity is a much stronger, firmer, and better place to start.

We all want to influence people. This influence should not be in a Machiavellian way, but rather with the idea of achieving a win-win. This mutual win is the bedrock of many relationships such as: Who should we date? Who might we select to be on our team? These types of decisions are built on trust. The most effective backbone of any communication is the answer to the question: "Does the communication come from a trusted source?" If not, the entire message is in doubt.

Harold Denton, who served as the president's representative to the nuclear incident at Three Mile Island was in the difficult situation of determining risks and handling the press. He offers this set of rules for managing any crisis with moral integrity:

1. Tell it like it is.
2. Admit uncertainties exist.
3. Don't make statements you'll have to retract later.
4. Act on the best estimate of a situation.
5. Refrain from "value judgments."

At a distinguished executive award ceremony in the White House Rose Garden, President Carter described how Denton's professional integrity helped overcome potential hysteria:

Harold Denton of the Nuclear Regulatory Commission has won wide praise for his performance following the Three Mile Island accident. When I went to the Three Mile Island plant the Sunday following the accident, I went into the control room with Harold, and from then on I saw on television every night his calm, professional, reassuring voice letting the American people know that they need have no fear.

Introducing former president Gerald Ford at Harvard, Senator Alan Simpson encapsulated the moral influence of integrity in President Ford's administration:

If you have integrity, nothing else matters.
If you do not have integrity, nothing else matters.

In Summary

Integrity is a powerful force.
Moral integrity is the bedrock of your reputation.
Either you have integrity, or you do not have integrity.

Listen Well

It is the business of the general to be quiet
and thus assure depth in deliberation.

—Sun Tzu

One doesn't think of any general as being quiet to assure depth in deliberation—certainly not General Patton, whom we see portrayed delivering famous lines in movies and on television.

But actually, many generals well understand the importance of being quiet. When General Curtis LeMay was repeatedly interrupted by a young lieutenant, he gently admonished the officer. The lieutenant responded that listening quietly was not how LeMay got to be a general. LeMay is reported to have answered the lieutenant, "No. But it *is* how I got to be a captain."

Engage in Active Listening

Good listening is an active process. It is how you can achieve the level of listening that Sun Tzu promises will "assure depth in deliberation."

Here are a few rules for active listening:

- *Play back what you are hearing.* The fundamental component of active listening is clarifying and confirming the other person's dialog with paraphrasing comments such as, "What I heard you say was . . ." or by simply repeating the

61

person's statement. This helps make sure you understood correctly and aids in getting additional information.

- *Ask questions.* Frequent questioning is another important component of active listening. Asking questions keeps you actively engaged, yields new information, and enables you to have a positive influence in the discussion. Be sincere with your questions and you will get more information flowing.

- *Acknowledge the other person's thoughts and feelings.* This engaging response can be with words or body language such as an occasional nod. Indications that you are receiving the commentary will help those talking to move past their own feelings and get to deeper issues. Conveying that you are indeed listening will help clear away the "baggage" others bring to the conversation. Acknowledging the "baggage" with a nod, or comment of understanding, can encourage him or her to move on in the conversation.

- *Focus on the other person's needs.* Listening provides information that enables you to build off the needs of others. If you can sincerely listen to and understand the needs of others, you are a powerful listener. The positive interactions of active listening give you a complete picture of the logic and emotion of the conversation. People will judge you to be empathetic.

- *Build the other person's self-esteem.* Smile, be helpful and positive. If you can be the kind of listener who builds the self-esteem of others, people will want to talk to you and feel comfortable confiding in you.

- *Be aware of your own listening "derailers."* Do you listen well to people whose values you do not share? Can you listen well to a variety of topics? Many things can affect our willingness to listen. If you know what derails you from listening well, you can achieve a more active listening stance.

- *Stay in the present.* A wandering mind is the opposite of good listening. Don't make assumptions or drift to future

implications of what you are hearing. Keep your mind
tuned to the present.
- *Take notes.* Whether or not you do anything with the notes,
taking them helps keep you focused on the conversation.

The Role of Questions

Listening in the present can be a challenge. The best way to keep active
in a conversation and influence the outcome is to ask questions.

Here are several benefits from properly worded questions:

- *Persuading.* Asking questions is a great way to help people
convince themselves of the right or wrong status of a
position. A question can make a point more clearly and
influence the other person more deeply than any statement
you make.
- *Staying engaged.* Asking questions helps both parties stay
engaged. Two-way conversations are always better than a
monologue. Asking questions keeps more of your brain
invested in listening.
- *Maintaining control.* Questions guide the discussion and
keep the conversation on track or lead in new directions.
When asking questions, you are in control. The person who
is in control wins.

People are more convinced by what they say than by what you say.
Don't expect immediate acceptance of your ideas. People are often
convinced more by time than by the truth.

Whenever executives ask my advice about how to prepare for an
important visitor, my response is "prepare a list of questions." Why is
it that we are always thinking of how we are going to respond and
what we are going to tell rather than what we are going to ask? Don't
play defense by responding to the other person's questions. A list of
questions prepared in advance is your strongest weapon.

In any conversation, the more the other person can tell you about his or her situation, the smarter you are. He or she knows you are smart because they delivered information to you. The more questions you ask, the more you listen; the more information you gather, the more you know.

Use the Power of Silence

Although questioning is a great tool, silence can be a powerful way to get the other person talking. Because we are uncomfortable with silence, we have a tendency to move into a conversation vacuum. Good salespeople know that when they ask a question that should be answered by the customer, the salesperson should "shut up" and wait, and wait, and wait for an answer.

Wait for the other person to respond. If you step into the vacuum first, you will not get the information you want. For example, if you ask a person if they will do something, give the other person time to think— the silence will often help pressure a positive response. If you talk first, you often give them an excuse for not taking action. For example, if you step into the conversation vacuum and say, "Perhaps you are too busy," the other person will often latch on to the excuse you offered and say, "That's right, I am just too busy." If you talk, you lose.

Sun Tzu encouraged his generals to be quiet "to assure depth in deliberation." Listening is a great tool to assure this depth and achieve the next level of personal success. By listening you get more information from each conversation.

In Summary

Listening is learning.
Practice active listening.
Questions provide the answer.

Be Considerate

*Pay attention to the soldiers' well-being
and do not fatigue them.*

*Try to keep them in high sprits
and conserve their energy.*
—Sun Tzu

Another translator points out how Sun Tzu's consideration for humanity extends beyond his own troops:

Treat the captives well, and care for them. Thus, command them with civility and imbue them uniformly with martial ardor and it may be said that victory is certain.

Although we usually do not find ourselves in this position of power over captives, a power hierarchy exists in many of our relationships. Our positions of "superior" power can range from hiring and firing, to whether we return phone calls, to the amount of the tip in a restaurant.

In these daily power relationships we are sometimes tempted to abuse our power and take advantage of the inherent inequality in the power balance. Whether consciously or subconsciously, we often make a decision that works to our advantage—perhaps not returning a phone call when we have nothing to gain. In one such example, the president of a large financial group bawled out one of his senior executives for making a delivery person wait in the lobby for twenty-five minutes to deliver lunch. The president knew that the waiting time reduced the delivery person's income. This incident became a corporate legend and solidified the president's reputation as a considerate person.

Sun Tzu's words about being considerate are appropriate for the way relative power in relationships shifts from situation to situation. The adage, "it's a small world" is relative to the issue. In the new "knowledge worker" information age, we sometimes find ourselves in control of information. At other times we are in need of information. Treating others with magnanimity when we are in control sets up the potential for a winning situation again when we are not in control.

Imagine the opposite scenario, where someone has alienated people across an industry. When that person goes to look for another job, is there a positive "buzz"? Also, as time goes on, alienated people rise to be peers or superiors. Often we run into these people in other parts of our life—at professional gatherings, a restaurant, or local school events. Don't burn bridges—ever.

Treating people well is a building block for the kind of success that sticks. The world is a series of complex relationships where we need to interact across industries and communities in a variety of roles. Being considerate of others, as Sun Tzu advises, will bring the most benefit.

In Summary

Don't abuse power.
Don't burn your bridges.
Do unto others as you
would have them do unto you.

Be Courageous

The principle of military administration
is to achieve a uniform level of courage.
—Sun Tzu

Sun Tzu's concern was getting his men to have the courage to engage in battle. We too have a need for courage in our everyday battles.

Everything we do involves risk. There is also risk in doing nothing. In fact, trying to maintain the status quo can be the greatest risk of all.

People who assume risk and take action seldom claim to be courageous. They talk about "just doing what anyone else would have done" in that situation. They do not profess any lifelong ambition to be courageous. When impulse is required they may say something like "I didn't think" or "it was the only thing to do." They simply did what they felt had to be done.

Build Self-Confidence

Confidence is the father of courage—taking action to do the right thing. We take action not just because of the impulse based on values but also because our training gives us confidence that we can succeed— or be mentally satisfied that we "gave it our best shot."

Self-confidence is great as long as it has a sound foundation. While lack of confidence is at one extreme of the scale, overconfidence is at the deadly other extreme. Overconfidence creates situations where you will be defeated by the unexpected. It's when we are sure everything is going well that we are in the most danger of being surprised.

Stevie Wonder put it this way:

When you begin thinking you are really number one, that's when you begin to go nowhere.

Physical self-confidence involves the body. Mental self-confidence involves the mind. In many cases, the physical and mental self-confidence generates mutual reinforcement. A quarterback who has learned to pass accurately, believes in his skill. The mental belief in his skill helps him keep a cool head and perform well on the field.

General Wavell said,

A bold general may be lucky, but no general can be lucky unless he is bold.

That is, we've got to have courage to take risks and if we do not take calculated risks we can't win. Concerning General McClellan at Antietam, biographer Stephen Sears writes of McClellan's cautious mindset stating that the general was:

. . . so fearful of losing that he could not win.

Put Courage into Action

Courage surfaces in many forms:

On September 11, 2001 in the sky over Pennsylvania, when Todd Beamer uttered the now famous "Let's roll," he and fellow passengers became heroes. They certainly did not board the plane planning to become heroes. Understanding the circumstances, they did what they needed to do. Trying to overtake the hijackers cost their lives, but it's very likely the crash in a Pennsylvania field saved lives at a target where the terrorists intended to crash the plane.

At the time Betty Ford was the First Lady of the United States, she was also secretly battling alcoholism. At first, she sought treatment confidentially. Eventually she demonstrated true courage by going "public" with her disease and founding the Betty Ford Center.

If courage is taking action, we all have the ability to be courageous. What we call courage is people taking action on something in which they believe.

Sun Tzu says,

He kicks away the ladder behind the soldiers when they have climbed up a height.

Climbing to success in life often requires having the courage to take a risk and kick away our own ladder.

However, courage must also be balanced with wisdom. Field Marshal Montgomery wrote:

Many qualities go to make a leader, but two are vital—the ability to make the right decisions and the courage to act on the decisions.

In Summary

Balance confidence with wisdom.
Take action to do the right thing.
This is courage.

Practice Discipline

If discipline is not enforced,
you cannot employ the troops.
—Sun Tzu

Some of *The Art of War's* most famous sections suggest strong discipline. The story of "the concubines" demonstrates how Sun Tzu uses discipline to achieve performance. This stress on discipline is consistent with winners everywhere.

Discipline Helps You Win

All great achievements are won through discipline. When home run king Henry Aaron was asked the difference between a good team and a great team his answer was one word, "discipline."

The Japanese have a word for the discipline of rebuilding a process—it's *kaizen*—meaning continuous improvement. *Kaizen,* as a discipline, also has its place in personal improvement.

After dominating the 1997 Masters, Tiger Woods studied videotapes of his performance, and went back to his coach to rebuild his swing so he could get even better! It's the discipline of continuous training and practice that makes Tiger Woods a champion among champions. He is known for being the last to leave the practice tee. Tiger excels—yet still improves—and so can we.

The day after being the youngest quarterback to win a Super Bowl and the second youngest to earn MVP honors, the New England

Patriots' Tom Brady exclaimed, "There's so much room for improvement, I don't know where to start."

Discipline is getting up early every morning to study how we can improve our profession—or exercise to improve our physical health. Mornings are best for practicing good discipline because putting "it" off until later in the day means that "it" can be put off until the next day, and the next day. Without consistency there is no discipline.

Discipline is a friend—not an enemy. *Excuses* for not practicing good discipline are the real enemy. Discipline keeps us doing the right thing and puts us on the path to achieving our goals.

Discipline Generates Power

In an overview of Colin Powell's "Seven Laws of Power," author Oren Harari identifies several of the General's key disciplines—perhaps Powell is a later-day Sun Tzu:

1. *Dare to be the Skunk.* Says Powell, "Every organization should tolerate rebels who tell the emperor he has no clothes . . ."
2. *To Get the Real Dirt, Head for the Trenches.* "The people in the field are closest to the problem. Therefore, that is where the real wisdom is." says Powell.
3. *Share the Power.* "Plans don't accomplish work. It is people who get things done." admonishes Powell.
4. *Know When to Ignore Your Advisors.* "Experts often possess more data than judgment" is Powell's view.
5. *Develop Selective Amnesia.* Powell says, "Never let ego get so close to your position that when your position goes, your ego goes with it."
6. *Come Up for Air.* Remarks Powell, "Anybody who is logging hours to impress me, you are wasting time."
7. *Declare Victory and Quit.* Powell advises about the importance of timing in withdrawing from a position.

Great rules! The problem is that following these rules, or any other set of rules, requires discipline. Self-discipline starts with doing small things that eventually become habits. Set a realistic number of goals. You can then move on to bigger challenges and more productive self-discipline that will generate increased success.

In Summary

Discipline is a friend.
Discipline makes good people great.
It takes discipline to practice self-discipline.

Be Creative

In battle, there are two kinds of postures,
extraordinary force and normal force.

Their combinations give rise to
an endless series of maneuvers.

—Sun Tzu

Another translator offers a view of the endless combinations that go into achieving creative results:

The musical notes are only five in number, but their melodies
are so numerous one cannot hear them all.
The primary colors are only five in number, but their combina-
tions are so infinite one cannot visualize them all.
The flavors are only five in number, but their blends are so var-
ious one cannot taste them all.

Increasingly, creativity of all sorts is recognized in popular culture.

Creativity is also important for managing our personal success. In the business world, new products have a "half life" of five years—that is, in five years, half of them will be obsolete. The success of most organizations results from a sustained succession of successful creativity—not a single product or lone creative effort. So, it is with the creativity of successful people.

Too often, we think of others, but not ourselves, as being creative.

Creativity is not a mystical thing; it is simply people searching for alternate solutions to problems. Creativity is a key component in our search for strategies for personal success.

Like so much of success in life, creativity appears to revolve around hard work, or "knowing our stuff." This is good news. Everyone has the opportunity to apply their own "creative genius" and tools in the search for success.

Unleash Creative Energy

Edward H. Land, the inventor of the Polaroid camera, explained the creative process this way:

> *True creativity is characterized by a succession of acts each dependent on the one before and suggesting the one after.*

Obviously, a path we can understand and follow. Darwin tells us the route is not easy. He says:

> *At no time am I a quick thinker or writer; whatever I have done in science has solely been by long pondering, patience, and industry.*

These descriptions of creativity do not suggest that great ideas come as "lightning bolts from the sky." Indeed, creativity involves rational advancements. Creativity arises out of what we know and the focus of our interests. Its fire is kindled by our passions.

A small Texas restaurant company constrained by their small lot size, looked for ways to grow their sales during the 1950s. Located on a busy thoroughfare, they searched for a creative way to get more business from the cars driving by daily and hung out a simple sign saying, "Drive Thru," a novel approach at the time. Their business exploded and others copied the idea. This creative idea has become so common we would be surprised to find a fast food restaurant that does not offer "Drive Thru" service.

Sun Tzu's quote on endless combinations is from a chapter in *The Art of War* titled "Energy." This energy is the creativity of human beings trying to be successful in tackling problems by looking for the extraordinary.

Sun Tzu's 2,500-year-old advice involves using simple weapons and limited resources. The extraordinary does not necessarily mean the newest and latest or the most expensive. Often the extraordinary lies in the simple, the mundane, the everyday things we look at with a fresh perspective. Sun Tzu suggests we tap into a creative reservoir of options others may not have considered.

Think Outside of the Box

We are all taught what is known, but we rarely learn about what is not known, and we almost never know about the knowable.
—Ralph E. Gormy

When the leader of an organization wanted to impress upon his people the need to search for the "not known" and "knowable," he drew a series of boxes on a flip chart:

He labeled the first box "Our Professional Expertise" and acknowledged that all had a high degree of knowledge.

Around the outside of that box, he drew another box labeled "Our Suppliers and Customers." He recognized a relatively high level of knowledge about this group.

Around these boxes, he drew another box labeled "Organizations in our Industry." Here, he expressed a concern about a lower level of knowledge by his people.

The next box encompassing all others was labeled, "Organizations Outside of our Industry." He expressed real concern about the existing level of knowledge.

The final box outside was labeled "Any Organization in the World" and further concern was expressed about the lack of knowledge.

He said, "Our task is to 'think outside of the box' and into new areas that enhance our value and assure future income. This requires getting out of the box and finding new opportunities away from the box."

Discovering new strategies outside of the box is not a case of "I'll know it when I see it," but rather: "I'll see it when I know it." That is, only when we know about *it* do we see *it* as a new opportunity.

Use the Tools of Creativity

If we understand that creativity is a thought process, enhanced by tools and aided by interaction, we can then understand how to use creativity to build our own personal success. Here are a few basic tools for creative thinking:

- On a "blank piece of paper" develop a list of options.
- Construct a "Ben Franklin Balance Sheet" by making two columns on a sheet of paper, heading one column "yes" and the other "no." Write down the "yes" and "no" reasons, compare them, and make your decision.
- Set up a structured brainstorming session where a small group gathers around a flip chart observing simple rules as they generate input. In one recorded instance of brainstorming, the group developed over 2,000 uses for parts of a chicken.

Most experts in creativity maintain that all of us are creative in our own way. In Sun Tzu's description it's the attainable creativity we all can achieve. It's not "inventing" new "musical notes," "colors," or "flavors." Creativity is simply combining the known in useful variations.

In Summary

Brainstorm.
Think outside of the box.
Unleash your creative energy.

Aim for High Standards

*The commander must create a helpful situation
over and beyond the ordinary rules.*

—Sun Tzu

Success is not doing what needs to be done. Success is going "above and beyond" what needs to be done. To succeed you must break "the ordinary rules" and set new standards of performance. Then you must break your own records.

What has been successful in the past, may continue to work in the future. But somewhere, sometime, someone will set a new standard of performance.

New standards result from changes in process. Examination of a century of records in the simple sport of the high jump reveals changes from the Scissors to the Western Roll to the Straddle to the Fosbury Flop. After the new and better methodology was introduced, no one could compete effectively with the old methodology. Today, every high jump champion uses the Fosbury flop. Tomorrow, who knows what the methodology will be. No one even knows whether that tomorrow is today or another day.

Look at the Process

When we think about excelling, we look at the results because that's where the measurement is made. However, it is the improvement in the *process* that creates the results.

Everything we do involves a process—a series of steps, a chain of activities. Building a fire is a process, preparing a meal is a process, and our work activities involve dozens of processes. In the performance of every process, we can identify three different types of standards:

- Input standards: Ingredients that go into a process.
- Operating standards: Process activities.
- Output standards: The results of the process.

For example, in preparing a meal

- Input standards determine the quantity and quality of the ingredients—to end up with a tender steak, you must have a good cut of meat; to make a good salad, you must have fresh ingredients.
- Operating standards determine the method of preparation—this is how long you cook the food and at what temperature.
- Output standards are concerned with the serving temperature, taste, and appearance of the meal.

Work Upstream

When thinking about preparing a meal, it's easy to see that input standards (ingredients) and operating standards (preparation) have a significant effect on the output standards (results). To achieve better results in any process, work upstream on input and operating standards.

To excel in any event requires a process of preparation and practice. A last-minute scramble to improve on the day of the event is too late. Only by improving the preparation and practice standards can we improve the results.

The higher the aim, the greater the stretch required to meet the standards, the more likely we are to achieve improvement.

Whatever you do, strive for the big changes in process that improve performance. These changes require more effort but they produce bigger rewards.

In Summary

Aim high.

Work upstream. Focus on process + ingredients.

Set new standards.

Seek Sound Counsel

Enlightened rulers must deliberate
on the plans to go to battle.
—Sun Tzu

As you develop plans and strategies for success, you can expect plenty of advice—often more than you want or need. Nevertheless, feedback from mentors and advisors who can give you ideas, support, and "course corrections" on your path to success is critical. Achievement is rarely accomplished in solitary practice without the aid of coaching.

Create a Counseling Staff

What you want from your staff of counselors is guidance that helps orient your internal compass to success. You will learn the most from people of good will who will be honest with you.

Listen carefully to your advisors and keep score of the usefulness of their advice. A few advisors of high reliability are more important than a large quantity of advisors.

Here are key counseling positions to fill:

- *A guru.* This is a wise person not directly involved in your activities who will listen and give good positive input. Gurus are traditionally sought out for their wisdom and can be great for exploring new ideas. With a good guru, one never feels threatened and is often inspired.

+adversaries

Info from adversaries tells you what they're thinking.

81

- *A coach.* While gurus are selected for overall wisdom, coaches know your profession or business. He or she can go beyond your own defenses and ego so you can truly "know yourself."

  What top professional athlete doesn't use a coach? Whether you are at the top of your profession, or on the way up, the tweaking and ideas from an outside coach can help raise the level of your success.

  Although you may not have access to a professional coach, the underlying idea of feedback from others can be applied—someone who can highlight the "blind spots" in your understanding or approach. A coach can be a friend who can help analyze what's happening and why. Mutual candor is the most valuable component of this relationship.

- *A sponsor.* This is someone at a high level in the organization who will act as your mentor. If that person moves on, cultivate another. One young man told me that about a year after he was hired, the three next senior people up the chain of command left. Since the young man had lost all of his original sponsors, he soon left the organization.

  Sponsors can also be valuable in outside activities. If asked to sit on a local board of a civic organization, ask the person inviting you to be your mentor in the workings of the team. This assistance can help you get up to speed faster, make you more effective, and deepen your relationship.

Beware of Eloquent Ignorance

I can recall a meeting at a consulting organization where several people were reviewing the content of a seminar. An individual who was visiting for the week was invited to the meeting. Wanting to exhibit his knowledge, he participated actively. His input, though well-intentioned, had little validity.

A room full of well-meaning people who have no knowledge of the situation will often come to the wrong conclusion. Eloquent ignorance yields deadly contributions.

I have found the easiest thing to do in any consulting situation is to give advice. Beware: good answers come only from a blend of prior experience and local knowledge.

Among people who know how to evaluate information flow, a common statement regarding an opinion is simply "that is one data point." This is a polite way of noting that "more than one data point" is needed to make an informed decision.

In his Tokyo headquarters, General MacArthur had a plaque with this quote from a Roman general:

In every circle and truly at every table there are people who lead armies into Macedonia. These are great impediments to those who have the management of affairs.

Follow these admonitions at your meeting tables:

1. The ability to carry on a meaningful and intelligent discussion decreases with an increase in the number of people attending.
2. All advice is not sound advice. All voices should not be considered equal. Keep counsel with advisors who know the situation.

The most frustrating meetings I attended were the twenty-two-person board of directors sessions of a national trade association. The group was too large for interchange and much advice was given by people impressed only with the sound of their own voices.

Avoid using meetings as a decision-making forum. Use meetings for input and *then* make your decision. Although it's good form to poll everyone in a small group to get their opinion, avoid voting. It polarizes people.

Small support groups of like-minded individuals, who may or may not be in your field, provide a good opportunity for exchanging information and networking. Noncompetitive relationships provide an ideal sounding board for testing ideas and solving problems.

In Summary

Quality beats quantity.
Eloquent ignorance is deadly.
Get a guru, a coach, and a sponsor.

Not always possible depending on your organizations.

Section Two
Strategies for Success

Introduction

Strategy Before
Tactics—Always

Strategy and tactics perform different roles in our quest for success.

- Strategy is thought seeking its means of execution.
- Tactics is the means to carry out the thought.

- Strategy determines the allocation of resources. It is the plan.
- Tactics deals with the use of resources. It is the implementation of the plan.

- Strategy is doing the right thing.
- Tactics is doing things right.

Compare the roles of strategy and tactics to a boat race. Strategy is the rudder—it determines direction. Tactics is the power that propels you to your goal.

Admiral Mahan in his work on sea power says:

Contact is a word which perhaps better than any other indicates the dividing line between tactics and strategy.

All planning activities are strategic; all implementation activities require contact and are tactical. For example, if your strategy is to find new employment by personally contacting people, your tactic is the process of making the actual contacts.

When the president of a company is determining the course of action, that activity is strategic. When the president of a company is talking to a customer, that action is tactical.

Action, any action no matter how seemingly small or insignificant, follows a plan or intention. Strategy is the creation of "right action." Strategy comes before tactics—always.

Know Your Battleground

One must compare the various conditions of the antagonistic sides in terms of the five constant factors:

1. Moral influence
2. Weather
3. Terrain
4. Commander
5. Doctrine

These five constant factors should be familiar to every general.

He who masters them wins; he who does not is defeated.

—Sun Tzu

The first step of great strategy is research—the gathering of information. The first section of this book is devoted to the most important area of information collection—knowing yourself.

Accurate information allows for better use of your resources. The information derived reduces risks because you have data that gives you better odds. Only a gambler with inside information can rationally bet his entire stake on a single race. What warnings we are going to get, we probably already have. Analysis of information available prior to the World Trade Center disaster proved that point once again.

Knowledge of a situation helps separate the useful from the useless. Your own interactive experience will help you evaluate the information.

The Boy Scouts say it most succinctly, simply "Be Prepared."

Seek Knowledge

In the first sentences of *The Art of War*, Sun Tzu says,

> *War is a matter of vital importance to the state; a matter of life
> and death, the road either to survival or to ruin.*
> *Hence, it is imperative that it be thoroughly studied.*

In the Griffith translation of *The Art of War*, the necessity of study
is emphasized by translating the word "imperative" as "mandatory"—
that is, "it is mandatory that it [war] be thoroughly studied." Knowledge is Sun Tzu's prime requisite to going to battle. He further advises:

> *Analyze the enemy's battle plan so as to have a clear under-
> standing of its strong and weak points. Agitate the enemy so as to
> ascertain his pattern of movement.*

Here are active ingredients that will help you build a strong knowledge base:

- *Learn your subject well enough to teach it.* The subject content is mastered if you feel able to teach it— a simple standard to establish. This search for expertise will make you
  ask deeper questions and anticipate questions that might be
  asked. Continuous searching for knowledge reveals new
  questions and information you did not know existed.
- Asking the "five why's" is a great way to get to the root
  cause of a problem. In the quality management arena where
  the "five why's" are considered an important tool, the questioning series might go like this:

  Q1. Why was the delivery late?
  A1. The delivery was late because the truck broke
  down.

  Q2. Why did the truck break down?

[handwritten margin note: Doesn't always work, evaluate When to use.]

A2. The truck broke down because it had not been lubricated.

Q3. Why wasn't the truck lubricated?
Q3. The driver had not been trained.

Q4. Why hadn't the driver been trained?"
A4. The training was canceled.

Q5. Why was the training canceled?
A5. The budget had been cut.

but is not always.

Now you are at the root cause of the problem. The late delivery was not caused by the driver, it was a result of a failure of funds to provide training on how and when to lubricate the truck.

If you can't ask and answer "why" five times, you probably haven't gotten to the heart of an issue.

- *Break your subject into pieces.* Sun Tzu often advises segmentation as means of study. Segmentation puts order in analysis. This is known as "eating the elephant" one bite at a time. Dissecting a subject into smaller units helps us understand each component and see how they meld into "the whole."

- *Study information close to time of use.* Because immediate application increases retention, training should take place close to time of use.

Or review

Expand Your Knowledge Horizons

but take it w/a grain of salt. You can burn out or get "analysis paralysis"!

Humorist-philosopher Mark Twain said,

I have never let my schooling interfere with my education.

This wise observation points us to widening our knowledge horizons. Limiting your knowledge to a narrow focus keeps you from seeing new and creative solutions. Leave yourself open to unexpected and perhaps unwelcome discoveries.

Here are a few ways to gain input beyond your area of operations.

- *Have a networking mindset.* Develop a network of bright people who can give you information that is important to your success. Know the thought leaders in your profession and in other areas of interest. Create situations where these people can be comfortable with you. Strive to be a contributor as well as a recipient of important information and your relationship will be secure.
- *Take advantage of learning opportunities.* Too many people claim they do not have time to attend trade shows or industry meetings (and not because they don't think they are important). This failure extends to volunteer organizations—such as, not attending the church council annual retreat. These people are saying they are "too busy chopping wood to stop and sharpen their ax." There never is enough time for all of the things we want to do. So concentrate your efforts. Take the time to learn something new. Do it now.
- *Spend time with people with different interests.* If you only spend time with people who know the same things you do, you won't learn new things. Even worse, you may become more certain that your information, ideas, and point of view are the most important or correct. Take courses in other fields; join organizations with other interests; go to a trade show in a different industry. You will gain new insights and find lots of new ideas to "steal" and apply.
- *Seek new experiences.* Don't let yourself get stuck in a rut! Explore the world; take a ride in a balloon; sign up for a raft trip; have new people over for dinner or attend a new civic activity.

- *Learn new questions.* Observing by wandering around is a good way to discover questions that need answers.

A recent consulting assignment in the grocery industry did not require me to visit any retailers, but I decided that on-site knowledge would be helpful. My travel schedule made it convenient to visit four of the five largest retailers—two of which are the most respected industry leaders. This hands-on experience enabled me to know the retail store component of the assignment better than anyone else. I arranged the information into a presentation for my client. He reported outstanding success—"kicked butt" was his exact phrase.

You are not in control of what challenges you will confront—you are in control of your response to those challenges. The broader your knowledge, the better your ability to react in a winning way to new challenges.

Sun Tzu writes:

The general who understands war is the controller of his
people's fate and the guarantor of the security of the nation.

To achieve his personal success, Sun Tzu studied war. The subject of your focus may be different. Your ability to affect your own personal success will be enhanced if you have access to many universes of knowledge.

In Summary

Know your stuff.
Expand your learning horizons.
Time invested in learning brings big rewards.

Build a Personal Network

Foreknowledge must be obtained
from men who know the enemy situation.
—Sun Tzu

Our existing network of friends and business associates is an outstanding source of "foreknowledge."

Sun Tzu says,

Those who do not use local guides are unable to obtain the
advantages of ground.

When we meet new people, we instinctively look for some common ground in order to establish a closer relationship; for example:

- At a conference in Helsinki, a Finnish manager told me how he searched America for a town to build his factory. Since the town he selected is my hometown, we developed a common bond.
- The stranger next to me at a luncheon turned into a friend when we discovered that we had been at the same New Year's Eve party.
- The passenger in the seat next to me on an airplane became an important contact when we discovered that both of us had lived in the same neighborhood in a distant city.

The foundation of your personal growth is the size and strength of your network. Chances are you probably do not have a very big or strong network unless you *actively* manage it. If you are too frugal about whom you call or the time you spend developing relationships, your network will be limited.

Tom Gunnels, author of *Keep Your Lights On,* gives good advice on the three types of knowledge critical to your success:

What you know!

Whom you know!

Who knows you!

Grow Your Network

A solid network grows from continuous investment of time and resources. It is a combination of new acquaintances and deep friendships. Good networking involves both meeting new acquaintances and actively moving these relationships to a closer friendship.

- *Set Contact Goals:* It's one thing to go to a meeting or conference and try to meet people; it's quite another to have a more specific goal in mind.

  The contact goal need not be large. Any reasonable goal serves as a gentle reminder to keep you moving from a comfortable circle of friends to seeking new relationships. If you do not feel a little uncomfortable when meeting new people and extending your network, you probably are not reaching enough people.

  Yes, the quality of contacts is important. However, I know of no one who has a high-quality network who also does not have a high-quantity network. As your contacts advance in their careers, they become high-quality resources—provided you keep in touch with them. That's the second part of networking—working the network.

  The Transition Team, an outplacement organization, offers the following goal-oriented advice for getting started on networking for a new job: "Make a list of the first twenty people you can think of who might be able to help you with your search. Don't be concerned with how comfortable you are calling upon them, or how long it has been since you have talked. List both the name and the person's relationship or role. For example: Mrs. Lawson—retired librarian (friend). Push yourself to reach the goal of twenty names! The next step is to inform your contacts of your situation in a positive way."

- *Solidify the Contact:* When you meet someone new, find out his or her interests and promise to send something he or she might like to have. For example, you might keep a file of interesting articles for this purpose. Get their business card, write down the promised action along with date and place you met. Then keep your promise to send something and be sure to include a handwritten note. Reason? A handwritten note is a personal touch and you want a personal relationship.

- *Use the Phone:* The telephone is an obvious networking tool. My traveling companions say that I've never been able to walk past a phone in an airport without using it. Their statement is quite accurate.

Whenever you place a call, it's in good taste to ask if he or she has a moment. Otherwise, you will be embarrassed by being cut short if the person is in the middle of a conference.

When I am contacting someone I do not know well (or at all), I never leave a message. This approach keeps me in control of my networking and solves several problems:

1. When I leave a message, I abrogate my right to call back because if the call isn't returned, then when is it appropriate to call again? If I do not leave a message, I can call anytime—even a few minutes later if I am told that my contact is on the phone.

2. Because I keep control of the time when the call is initiated, I can call when I am mentally prepared.
3. I avoid the embarrassment of receiving a return call and not remembering why I called.

- *Use the Internet:* A great networking tool if you use it wisely. Keep messages brief and informative.

Keep Your Network Active

Be active. The more people you know and the more friendships you cultivate, the more people you will know well. Some of your contacts—hopefully, many—will breed other contacts.

When you plan to visit a city, call people in your network and ask to meet them. Your contacts will be flattered by your interest. Whether or not you do meet, the offer breeds a stronger relationship.

In some cities, I've had three breakfasts with three different groups of people—although you need to watch your diet, there is no rule against this. A friend facetiously commented that the way to "do New York" is to plan three lunches on the same day. Because many New Yorkers commute, breakfast or dinner meetings are inconvenient.

The bad news about networking is the continuous investment of time and energy. The good news is that it is fun and generates results.

Statisticians say only four contact links separate you from anyone in the world. That is, if you know the name of the person you want to reach. And, if you don't? What if you are looking for someone who can help you solve a problem and you do not know precisely who that person is? Then you really need a network—and the broadest base yields the best responses.

In Summary

Set stretch goals.
Solidify every contact.
Actively work your network.

Develop Great Strategies

*Their aim must be to take all under heaven intact
through strategic superiority.*

—Sun Tzu

Another translator of *The Art of War* describes in very simple terms that winning strategy achieves victory before the battle:

*A victorious army seeks its victories before seeking battle.
An army destined to defeat fights in the hope of winning.*

Without strategy, success is left to chance. With strategy, we have direction and goals.

Tactical considerations can influence your strategic plan. You may need to direct your efforts in an area that is tactically possible, instead of one that is strategically preferable. Financial or family considerations will influence your selection of strategic goals. You may want to be president of the United States; however, a high political office may be a more practical goal.

It is a fundamental truth that the strategy must be correct to succeed in any endeavor. There's no chicken and egg problem here. The strategy must be right first; then the tactics can support the strategy. Excellent strategy can sustain many tactical failures.

A bad strategy supported by good tactics can be a fast route to failure. Sustained tactical success—even continuous brilliant execution of tactics—seldom overcomes an inadequate strategic posture.

The best personal strategies cascade from a vision of the future. The vision is not a flash of insight. It requires the sweat equity of careful consideration.

Have a Vision

A "vision" is not just a vision statement. Visions are not words, they are discoveries of "what we will be." Without a vision, we perish mentally. A friend who headed a consulting organization stated clearly that:

Visions are the vehicles that transport us across the boundaries of current reality to the boundless hopes of a future seemingly beyond our grasp. What once we deemed impossible becomes not only possible but probable when we live out our vision through actions.

Here are guidelines for establishing a vision of your success.

1. *Identify your core competencies.* What is it that others say you do best? What do you like to do? Ask trusted advisors to comment on your identification of core competencies.
2. *Determine applications.* Think about how you can be most productive using these core competencies. Where can you best apply your talents and skills?
3. *Establish a direction.* Develop a clear mind-picture of where you want to go and what you want to be. Explore factors critical to achieving your vision.

Express the Vision as a Vivid Image

A vivid image is an energetic and vibrant description of what your world would look like if your vision was achieved or manifested.

Transform your mission into word pictures:

Write a vivid image of your vision in a single session. Start with a sentence like "Five years from now I will . . . " and let thoughts flow out of your head and onto a sheet of paper. Continue without stopping until you have covered several sheets of paper. Set your comments aside for a day or two and then simplify this vivid image into a short paragraph or two. The mental exercise is more important than the words on paper. Now you are ready to transform the vision into action.

The value of exploring the vision is in the mental exercise. The process of exploring crystallizes your thoughts and takes you one step closer to realizing your mission.

Develop Personal Strategic Initiatives

A strategic initiative is strategy on paper. In a few words, the strategic initiative provides your compass and states your goals.

Think about existing opportunities. Review threats and blockers to your vision. Consider optional courses of action. Then write out your strategic initiatives using statements like the following:

> *Career:* I will get a degree at night school that makes me eligible for promotion.
> *Family:* I will send our children to college.
> *Renewal:* I will go on an educational trip overseas for a week.
> *Health*: I will train and attempt to run a marathon.

Now, move on to implementation. Prioritize the most important three to five initiatives. Do not select more than this number or you will be attempting too much. Develop a plan of action for each initiative. Be diligent in your follow-through. These steps will ultimately create your individualized pathway to personal success.

In Summary

Develop a vision.
Express as a vivid image.
Drive success with strategic initiatives.

Win Without Fighting

*To win 100 victories in 100 battles
is not the acme of skill.*

*To subdue the enemy without fighting
is the supreme excellence.*

—Sun Tzu

That offensive strategy should be aimed at winning without major conflict is a principle often repeated throughout *The Art of War*.

Find Victory in Your Strategy

Your strategy should be so good that you will not have any competition; if you do encounter able opponents, your tactics should be so good you will win anyway.

It is in the formulation of strategy that victory is determined. The person who wins will probably be the person who has already won. That is, the winner will have developed a great strategy prior to engaging the opponent.

Those who win without fighting are often so well prepared to fight and win that they avoid battle by intimidating their opponents. The potential opponent decides to expend his or her energy elsewhere because they are afraid of losing or do not like the cost of winning.

Phillip Fulmer, national-championship-winning football coach, at the University of Tennessee says,

I constantly coach our players about having the intensity to be able to intimidate our opponents. This doesn't mean to play outside the rules. It means that our players should be fundamentally sound and in such good physical condition that they can outlast and outwork their opponents.

In this sense, Coach Fulmer is talking about being so good that our performance is, in itself, intimidating.

In every part of Switzerland are streets, plazas, and statues honoring generals of an army that did not fight. Switzerland wins a lot of wars (that it never fought) using the Porcupine Strategy:

You
roll up into
a ball in place and
brandish your
quills.

The Swiss army is composed of many hundreds of thousands of civilians who train regularly and keep weapons in their home. Switzerland does not have an army; Switzerland is an army.

Sun Tzu reinforces his belief in the strength of strategy by saying:

Those skilled in war subdue the enemy's army without fighting. They capture the enemy's cities without assaulting them and overthrow his state without protracted operations.

Capture the Strength of Innovation

Sun Tzu says that if you are not doing something unique, you have not really attained a victory:

To foresee a victory no better than ordinary people's foresight is not the acme of excellence.
Neither is it the acme of excellence if you win a victory through fierce fighting and the whole empire says, 'Well done!'

Sun Tzu goes on to confirm that easy wins are not victories. The real victories are where you "conquer an enemy already defeated" (by strategy).

Innovation often gives you the kind of strength that, in itself, declares victory. Winners innovate to find new ways to victory without encountering competition; for example, the youngster entering a science fair with an exhibit that is clearly at a higher level than other students. Think of Dick Fosbury innovating the Fosbury Flop in the high jump, or Dell selling computers direct to customers and ignoring traditional distribution channels.

Thinking up new ideas is easy; the test for success lies in the ability to implement the ideas. Here are steps that will help energize your mind to see a different reality and find new possibilities.

1. *Define the challenge.* Use words or draw pictures to state essential elements of the challenge. For example, Fosbury wanted to jump higher so that he could win competitively.

2. *Develop "How about . . ." statements.* These statements should lead you to the radical and unusual. Go beyond the boundaries of the normal. Fosbury's statements might have been:

   - How about using a different type of pole?
   - How about using a pogo stick?
   - How about a different take-off style?
   - How about radically changing the way I go over the bar?
   - How about talking to other coaches?
   - How about looking at the techniques of divers?
   - How about being shot out of a cannon?

3. *Visualize action.* Select several ideas that are intriguing and visualize putting them into action. Imagine what happens, moment by moment. Focus your interests on the action, not the results. Observe what is interesting as the scene takes place.

4. *Innovate.* Diagram input from these ideas and look for a new way to fulfill the challenge.

A successful biologist said,

Discovery consists of seeing what everybody has seen—and thinking what nobody has thought.

Among the orchards of Northern Michigan, Bob Sutherland saw what everybody has seen—cherries—and thought what nobody has thought. The result: his unique store is themed around a fictitious nation—the Cherry Republic. Today, in the tiny town of Leelanau, shopping is fun among the décor spoofing the fictitious Cherry Republic. Here throngs of tourists choose from hundreds of cherry-related products.

In Summary

Great strategy is better than great combat.
Innovations yield great strategies.
Great strategy wins.

孫子

Apply Strength Against Weakness

The law of successful operations is to
avoid the enemy's strength and strike his weakness.

—Sun Tzu

Concentration of strength is one of the major principles of military success—and of success in any endeavor. Every successful attack has succeeded because somebody concentrated.

Concentration is not a mere mass of numbers, but rather the focusing of strategy and tactics where you want to win. The key to success is not how much strength you have, but how and where you concentrate your power.

Use Many to Strike the Few

Although more than two millennia of time and thousands of miles separate Sun Tzu from the European general, Carl von Clausewitz, look at the following similarity of advice.

If we are able to use many to strike few at the selected place,
those we deal with will be in dire straits.

—Sun Tzu
Fifth century B.C.

Where absolute superiority is not obtainable, you must produce a relative one at the decisive point by making skillful use of what you have.

—Carl von Clausewitz

A.D. nineteenth century

Although some suspect that Clausewitz could have read *The Art of War*, there is no proof that this happened. It is clear that Sun Tzu's Eastern strategy and Clausewitz's Western strategy agree on concentrating strength against weakness. Sun Tzu says to concentrate "at the selected place." Clausewitz says concentrate "at the decisive point." Clausewitz further admonishes that this tactical concentration must be achieved by "making skillful use of what you have"—definitely the situation facing most of us.

Find a Weakness

Again, Sun Tzu says,

His offensive will be irresistible if he plunges into the enemy's weak points.

People recognized for expertise have concentrated their quest in a narrow area where the weakness is lack of competition.

Dan Poynter earned his reputation as an expert in sky diving by jumping from an airplane over the North Pole and then writing a book on the subject. Poynter parlayed his book success into recognition as a "how to" expert.

Jim King parlayed his corporate specialty in analyzing environmental risk into a position of expertise by writing the 1,290-page *Environmental Dictionary*. From this base he launched a new consulting career.

You are not aware of Poynter's expertise unless your are into sky diving or publishing. Likewise, King's fame is confined to the world of environmental management. On any street in every town are niche entrepreneurs who are "experts" in narrowly defined areas where there is limited competition—or none at all.

The essence of the daily task of winning is to operate from a base of relative superiority in a specific field. That is, you must select a niche where you can apply your strengths against weaknesses.

When you think about where you are going to concentrate, look for the weakness of your opponent's strength. For example, in 1704, Peter the Great arrived at the Russian town of Dorpat to assist 20,000 Russians who had forty-six cannons firing at the besieged garrison. He found his commander's concentration faulty. They were firing at the town's strongest bastions. Peter switched the artillery to the most vulnerable walls and a breach was made for Russian troops to enter. Victory came five weeks after the siege began but only ten days after Peter arrived to focus the strength of his cannons against the weakest walls.

Obtain Relative Superiority

Organizational Superiority: Often we can obtain a relative superiority with an organizational strength. That is how the Greeks fighting in a phalanx won the Battle of Marathon against the Persians who were fighting one to one.

Organizational superiority is what helps sports teams win, and makes business franchises successful. Organizational superiority is achieved by any individual who marshals his or her personal resources—often known as "getting your ducks in a row."

Technological Superiority: Another avenue to relative superiority is through technology. Today, this winning strength is most often found in hi-tech organizations. Each of us can derive the advantages of applying the latest technological knowledge in our chosen areas of endeavor.

It's critical to keep up with the rapid pace of change in technology. Distinct advantages accrue to those who keep on the leading edge. Not only can technology help you look like a leader, it can help you be a leader. People want to associate with knowledgeable leaders.

Reinforce Strength—Not Weakness

The best odds for success are achieved by spending time, money, and energy reinforcing what is working. Then you are leveraging off what you do well.

When you spend time and resources shoring up what's not working, you are reinforcing weakness—this is diametrically opposed to the concept of reinforcing strength.

It's not that you shouldn't pay attention to weak areas, the problem is that reinforcing weakness denies time and resources to areas of strength. The best results are obtained when strengths are reinforced.

A regular system of deliberately and continuously reinforcing strength is alien to many organization cultures. Too often, managers think they must be involved in day-to-day operations. Because they get so involved in giving support to the weak, they end up defending instead of attacking.

In the world of success, coaches coach and players play. When coaches try to play and players try to coach, the results can be disastrous.

The key to success is making sure that all resources are focused on predetermined strategic initiatives. A military adage warns:

> *Guns that have not fired, have not attacked, no matter how long they have been in position.*

In Summary

Know your strengths.
Concentrate strengths against weaknesses.
The concentration is always at a decisive point.

Avoid the Avoidable

*By taking into account the unfavorable factors,
he may avoid possible disasters.*

—Sun Tzu

Victory and success go not always to the most brilliant, but to those who make the fewest mistakes. This task is not easy; mistakes are often visible only in hindsight.

The process of avoiding the avoidable is one of understanding that physical hazards are identifiable obstacles concerning which specific measures can be taken. In contrast, the human element is completely unpredictable. Consequently, you must take specific action to reduce the possibility of defeat by physical conditions in order to devote your full resources to dealing with the unpredictable human elements.

Here are examples of how to avoid the avoidable and increase the odds of attaining success:

Schedule regular training that increases your professional skills
or prepares you for an alternate career.
Always arrive early for appointments so that you do not have
to begin with the negative of an excuse for being late.
Understand that every document presented to another has
both form and substance. Go for the ultimate quality in
the physical element of form so that it does not distract
from the more psychological and important elements of

substance. For example, errors in spelling and language usage can detract from the content of any presentation.

In your work life, avoid the avoidable by never allowing your plan to fail because of quality of the product or service, or delivery time, or any physical element.

There are many other simple rules to follow in everyday life that can keep us from disasters—large and small. Here are a few:

Take an aspirin prior to a long plane flight and walk around during the flight to reduce the risk of blood clots—known as economy class syndrome.

Never send a letter on the day you write it. An amazing amount of wisdom results from the passage of time and a second look.

Carry two credit cards in different places. If you lose one, you have another.

Don't drink and drive.

In Summary

Correct predictable components first.
Then devote resources to the unpredictable.
Sloppy form destroys the content of substance.

Build a Strong Position

*It is a doctrine in war that we must rely on the fact
that we have made our position invincible.*

—Sun Tzu

Our personal strength is the foundation of our position. It encompasses the way we act and what we do best.

We perceive our position by the way we see ourselves. Others perceive our position by the way they see us.

The perception is indeed the reality.

We can change ourselves and we can cause a change in the way others perceive us. Although our actions can change our position, the change is permanent only if our actions are "for real." Attempts at false positioning are destructive.

We are all actors on the stage of life. Our best role is to act out our part based on who we really are. One of the greatest compliments I've heard about another person is, "He is who he says he is!"

Today, our position is determined by what we do with the strengths we have. Tomorrow, our position is determined by how well we have applied our strengths today. Strong positions provide stability and direction to life. Weak positions are destructive.

Find Strength in Relationship Positions

Wheatly and Kellner-Rogers in their book, *A Simpler Way*, make a strong true statement:

Relationships are all there is.

A position with strong relationships is an invincible position.
Here are the major positions one can occupy in life's families:

Home family position: For married persons, the nuclear family is well defined by marriage or birth. For singles, the surrogate family often is a circle of friends. For all, our family includes some circle of close relatives who give support. How we fulfill our roles determines our ability to contribute to the strength of the family and receive strength from it.

I recall a young lady telling me that she worked every day on being happily married. Like our job at work, our home life requires that we practice the give-and-take of making our relationships successful.

Religious family position: To many, this position is much more than a Sunday thing. Religion can be a great source of position strength. It is the only strength that stretches into infinity. Of all strengths, it is the most deeply personal.

Career family position: The educational process points us to a career position. In careers, there is a ladder that can be climbed and climbing the ladder determines the goals for new positions—or we may choose to move to a different career ladder.

"Other interests" family position: This is what we do in our spare time beyond family, religion, and work. This position may be intertwined with, and supportive of, other positions. For example, a parent (nuclear family) may coach a child's sport (other interest's family).

In each family, you need to devote time and energy to your role; when you excel in the role, your position becomes invincible.

Clearly Define Your Position

To be perceived as more than just another person, develop a personal brand. Define that brand identity narrowly so you can own it. For example, "The author who writes mystery stories involving black Persian cats."

A key to discovering your personal "brand identity" is to imagine a good friend, with a sense of humor, introducing you to an audience using a descriptive middle name. What is the middle name that describes your major interest or area of expertise? That is your personal brand identity.

Reinforcement of a position is possible only after you clearly determine what that position is. This reinforcement is an evolving process.

For example, when I decided to become an expert on the application of military strategy to business, I spent time between appointments and in the evenings visiting bookstores and libraries to find books on the subject.

I climbed over students reading in the aisles of bookstores in Cambridge, Massachusetts. I visited the Library of Congress as well as stores specializing in military books. I gained access to military libraries at West Point and the Infantry school at Fort Benning. Every city I visited offered new opportunities for expanded knowledge in my chosen field of concentration. I applied the knowledge of military strategy to my first book: *Winning the Marketing War.*

I developed a platform presentation on the application of military strategy to business. Eventually, I addressed audiences on five continents on the application of both Eastern and Western military strategies. When I spoke at seminars, I met other prestigious speakers and broadened my world of contacts. The national network became an international network. My credentials provided access to business and military leaders who provided an information flow in my chosen field of expertise.

During my search for information on military strategy, I redefined my focus to accumulating expertise about one specific Chinese strategist—Sun Tzu. The only place in the world where you can find every English translation of *The Art of War* is in my personal library.

Almost every success I experience today can be traced to contacts from my quest to becoming an expert in the application of military strategy to business. When asked if I achieved that goal, my answer is, "Probably not, but I am still learning and improving from life's new experiences."

In the course of this journey to expertise, I twice visited China to understand the Chinese view of Sun Tzu's lessons and lecture on my views of applying Sun Tzu's philosophy.

When the opportunity arose for me to consult internationally, I set another goal of developing expertise on the differences in service quality around the world. Since I would be staying at some of the finest hotels in the world, I decided to interview the general managers of these hotels. These professionals are a knowledgeable source of information because hotels are the world's stage for service quality. The interviews yielded valuable insights on service quality and served as a basis for my book, *Building Bridges to Customers*.

Here are a few rules for building expertise:

1. *Select a particular niche.* The narrower the field, the more limited the competition.
2. *Support your native expertise.* Develop expertise in an area that reinforces your current strengths. Anything else is a hobby.
3. *Be an explorer.* Get out of town and meet new people. Network. Go to the source.
4. *Build a reputation.* Experts aren't chosen, they are announced. Be your own announcer.

5. *Get more expertise.* The quest never ends.
6. *Answer the phone.* You know you are arriving when people start calling you.

Form Alliances

Get allies to help secure your position. This is where networking and teamwork unite to generate personal power. Spending time with others who have similar interests opens the opportunity for new knowledge.

You can't do it all. Every golf professional has a coach, an agent, and a caddie—who does much more than carry his clubs. Get a coach, empower agents, and find other advisors who can discuss the approach for each shot at a better life.

Don't be a bore, but do use every opportunity to communicate about your chosen position. The Internet puts you in touch with the world.

Warning!

It's an axiom that the more secure you feel about your position, the greater the danger. It is when you feel most secure that you become most vulnerable to surprise.

In Summary

Be who you really are.
Build sound relationship positions.
Strengthen expertise to strengthen your position.

Organize a Team

When the troops are united,
the brave cannot advance alone,
nor can the cowardly retreat.
—Sun Tzu

Determined to succeed, we are too often focused on applying our own skills to solving a problem. We jump from "our idea" to implementing "our solution" without soliciting assistance. We have been conditioned to work as individuals, not as team members.

Form Teams to Win

To make the point about how teams succeed, I often use the following exercise in workshops:

I ask people to count the number of times the letter *f* appears in the box labeled "f" Exercise.

Try it for yourself now. Count the number of times you see the letter *f*. Do this before you read the answer in one of the following paragraphs.

"f" Exercise

The necessity of training farm hands for first-class farms in the fatherly handling of farm livestock is foremost in the minds of farm owners. Since the forefathers of the farm owners trained the farm hands for first-class farms in the fatherly handling of farm livestock, the farm owners feel they should carry on with the family tradition of training farm hands of first-class farms in the fatherly handling of livestock because it is the basis of good fundamental farm management.

Count the number of "f"s in this exercise.

Often, participants will offer a wide range of answers ranging from the low-twenties to the mid-thirties. As responses are solicited, the audience chuckles because it seems ridiculous that such a simple question could have so many different answers. Yet, when participants completed the exercise, they were certain they had the correct answer.

Participants are then asked to work in small teams of three or four individuals to determine the correct answer. Usually, someone on each team suggests that one person count the number of *f*s on a specific line. Often, every team now gets the right answer—proving that better results are arrived at by working together as a team than trying to solve problems as individuals. Because these individuals have determined a team process for getting the correct answer, they now have the tools to get a correct answer on a similar exercise. (The correct answer is 39.)

We cannot achieve the level of success as individuals that we can as members of a team. We cannot compete as individuals against others who are functioning as a team.

Some may think that time consumed in teamwork is inefficient. So is defeat.

About 100 years ago, a French strategist stated the value of teams:

Four brave men who do not know each other will not dare attack a lion. Four less brave, knowing each other well, sure of their reliability and consequently of mutual aid, will attack resolutely. This is the science of organization of armies in a nutshell.

—Ardant du Picq

Knowing others well and being sure of reliability and mutual aid is the essence of teamwork in a nutshell. Successful teams are made up of people who know and trust each other. To operate effectively as a team, members must spend time learning team skills and working together as a team. It takes time to build the productive interaction and mutual trust of a team. Successful teams are not made up of people who have been lectured to about teamwork; successful teams are made up of people who have shared experiences working towards a common goal.

Bo Schembechler, as football coach at the University of Michigan, said,

> *You will never get the same effort from one man seeking glory as from a group of men pulling for a shared goal.*

Share a Common Purpose

Being involved in a common, unifying purpose energizes and excites us towards a goal. A purpose helps us commit with our hearts and not just our heads. Sun Tzu advises *he whose ranks are united in purpose will be victorious.* Building towards a common purpose has a lot to do with how "who we are" is integrated into our personal style. This spirit of common purpose builds team consistency. Teams of motivated, mature people will accomplish amazing things.

In Summary

Form teams.
Share a common purpose.
Working together gets better answers.

Go for a Breakthrough

Use the normal force to engage;
use the extraordinary to win.

—Sun Tzu

Nowhere does the simplicity of Sun Tzu's ancient wisdom ring more clearly than in the advice of employing the extraordinary to win.

Strive for a Big Win

Thinking big helps focus your strategy on meaningful gains. It's not that small goals are not important; it's that the best small goals are steps to a larger goal. In life, we tend to lose interest in small goals that do not lead to major results.

Little victories can be just as time consuming as the big victories. Wherever you are going, plan a strategy that achieves a big goal.

It is easy to do a lot of nice things. The real issue is to focus your energy where you can make a difference.

Years ago, when General MacArthur headed the American Olympic Committee, he advised the athletes, "We are here to represent the greatest country on earth. We did not come here to lose and lose gracefully, we came to win and win decisively."

With these few words, MacArthur took advantage of the opportunity to merge a big responsibility, representing America, with a big goal, winning decisively. Inherent in supporting most big goals is the opportunity to declare an energizing reason for justifying the effort.

Eighteenth-century strategist, Carl von Clausewitz, stated simply:

Only great battles produce great results.

A supporting corollary would be:

Only the prospect of great results can produce the means to fight great battles.

It's the prospect of great results that generates great enthusiasm.

Plan Breakthroughs

Often, we attempt to achieve breakthroughs by searching for more resources—if only we had more time, more funds, or more support in our projects. We fail to recognize that "just a little more" is not enough. As we achieve incremental increases, so do our opponents. The result of two opposing forces inputting the same amount of energy is another stalemate with no clear winner. The cycle repeats with each exerting "a little more effort" thus creating another standoff. The problem is "just a little more" doesn't work.

Too often we ignore the strategist who advised:

Do not renew an attack along the same line (or in the same form) after it has once failed.

The message is: Trying harder is not the solution, trying *smarter is*. Breakthroughs don't simply happen, they are planned.

Generals say that in order to win in war, you must:

Dislocate the enemy and exploit that dislocation.

Think of battles as mental ones where you must capture mind-share for your idea, service, or product. Disrupting the mind gets the other person's attention. To gain mindshare, think of how you can disrupt the mind and then intrude into that disruption.

The disruption cannot be crass or obnoxious. It must be in good taste. However, to break through the clutter, our message must disrupt the mind—that is, we must gain attention.

When I wanted to sell a product licensed with the Pink Panther brand name, I gave away six-foot-high stuffed Pink Panthers as premiums with the purchase of a quantity of the product. The sheer size of the Panther was disruptive. The intrusion was achieved by appealing to the desire to own this unique item. Everyone wanted a six-foot Pink Panther as a gift for a child and the more children you had, the more Panthers you needed, and the more products you needed to purchase to get the Pink Panther. Wow! A breakthrough.

I've used a messenger to deliver six-foot Pink Panthers with a pink tag reading, "You'll be tickled pink with the opportunity I have for you." (signed) Gerald Michaelson. The recipient may never have heard my name, but that's okay because I'm not asking him to call. I initiate a phone call a few days later and identify myself. Responses from the receptionist have been comments like, "He wants to talk to you." That is the introductory atmosphere I wanted to create. The next step is to intrude into that disruption with a personal visit and a benefit-laden message. Wow! A breakthrough.

When a person who received informational material from me could not recall receiving the material, I sent the brochures again in a box with a chocolate chip cookie the size of a pizza. The message written in frosting on the cookie said, "Here's the cookie with the message." When I called again, the lady said, "You made my day. When are you coming to see me?" Wow! Another breakthrough.

When I wanted to promote a book dealing with the problems of business overcapacity, I sent twenty-five different boxes of chocolate-chip cookies to business writers—along with a copy of the book. When my newest product was featured in a contest on the back of a Kellogg's cereal package, I sent every salesperson a case of the cereal to pass out to retailers selling the product. Wow! More breakthroughs.

When a young man in Australia wanted to apply for a job with an advertising agency whose principal client sold athletic clothing, he didn't just send his resume. He got a "foot in the door" by arranging with the building custodian to wedge a running shoe in the owner's office door one morning with his resume and an appropriate message. He got the interview and the job. Wow! Another breakthrough.

At a national trade show, I arranged to stack a display of one million dollars in one-dollar bills to illustrate a profit opportunity. Objections from a few nay-sayers disappeared when the company president declared in favor of the promotion. The money was banded together in packages of one thousand dollar bills, stacked seventy-two bills high, and fourteen bills wide in a glass case that towered high in the air. The effort was costly, but the resulting increase in sales was overwhelming—we tripled the sale volume. Wow! A breakthrough.

As orders poured in and results became evident, no one inquired about the cost. Proof that great efforts produce big wins and the strength of big wins overpowers criticism. Incremental improvements are important; the big win comes when you plan for a breakthrough.

Use Extraordinary Effort

Extraordinary effort generates extraordinary results. Sun Tzu says,

To a commander adept at the use of extraordinary forces, his resources are as infinite as the heaven and earth, as inexhaustible as the flow of the running rivers.

The reference to infinite resources simply means the creative mind can find an inexhaustible variety of ways to do the extraordinary.

In Summary

Be pleasantly disruptive to capture attention.
Be intrusive with real benefits.
Go for it big-time.

Have a Plan

The commander who gets many scores
during the calculations in the temple before the war
will have more likelihood of winning.

—Sun Tzu

Too often, planning is simply a mental process. An idea that is only in our head as we simply look at the past and adjust for the future. Sailors call this "steering by the wake."

In war, generals say that no plan survives the first battle. The same is often true in life—outside events influence the success of our plan. Do not let this possibility of disruption defer you from planning. Without a plan of action, you may never get started. Simply consider plans as a basis for change. President Harry Truman said,

> *When I make a dumb decision, I go on and make another dumb decision.*

Put Your Plan in Writing

The plan exists *only* when it is a written document. If you do not have a plan in writing you may have a dream, a vision—or perhaps a nightmare. You do not have a plan *unless* it is a written document.

Kipling wrote:

> *I have six honest serving men.*
> *They taught me all I knew.*

Their names were what and where and when,
And why, and how, and who.

Answer the questions posed by the six honest serving men and you have a simple format for putting your plan into writing.

Why am I taking this course of action?
What am I going to achieve?
How am I going to proceed?
When am I going to do it?
Where will it happen?
Who is going to be involved?

It's so easy to answer these questions in our head and so much better to put the answers in writing. Tom Monaghan, founder of Domino's Pizza, says,

Writing is the key to my system. I carry a legal pad with me everywhere I go. All my thoughts, my plans, my dreams, and my analyses of problems are written down in my pad. I sometimes have several pads going at once for different kinds of thoughts. I have accumulated dozens of these pads—although I never look at them again. What's important is the thinking that goes into the writing, not the words that wind up on paper. I set long-range goals, annual goals, monthly, weekly, and daily goals. The daily goals take the form of to-do lists. The long-range goals are dream sheets.

Instead of Monaghan's yellow pad, I prefer an attractive bound journal that can be purchased for $10 at a bookstore. Others prefer notebook planners with calendar pages. Whatever you use, a single place to record everything is the kind of organization that will make you more productive.

Adapt to Circumstances

Your plan must be flexible and adaptable to circumstances. A plan like a tree must have branches if it is to bear fruit. A plan without options is like a barren pole.

Sun Tzu says:

Tactics change in an infinite variety of ways to suit changes in the circumstances.

No single plan works well for everyone and everywhere. If your plans are too rigid, you will not be able to adjust to circumstances. Planning is a process of understanding what is happening in constantly changing situations and adapting with energy and determination.

The intuition that breeds great strategies and great plans can only come from being in touch with the situation. Your planning cannot be done in a vacuum. The winning plan incubates in the warmth of knowledge of where you want to go and how you are going to get there.

Moses brought down from the mountain just ten commandments to live by. The U.S. Army sets forth only nine principles of war. At Gettysburg, Abraham Lincoln's speech lasted less than ten minutes. Often, very often, less is more. Your plan for success does not need to be complicated. A simple plan is easier to translate into action.

Here are three simple, basic rules for implementing your plan.

1. *Set a goal and timetable.* Although you cannot be number one in everything, you can be number one in something.
2. *Get started.* The greater your initiative, the greater your momentum, and the faster your journey to success.
3. *Leverage every gain.* Use each success to attain the next level.

Develop a contingency plan to provide for the next step following a success or failure. Good planning considers the alternatives available. Don't rely on crystal-ball assumptions. Examine the worst that can happen and provide for such a contingency. Frederick the Great said,

There is no dishonor in a hard fought defeat and no excuse in being surprised.

In Summary

Think of every plan as a plan of action.
Planning without acting is a waste of time.
Acting without planning is a recipe for defeat.

Section Three
Tactics for Success

Introduction

Coordinate Tactics
with Strategy

In any hierarchy, strategy at one level will often be tactics at the next level. That is how the master plan becomes increasingly more focused as action cascades through an organization.

Strategy and tactics must be woven together. When we separate planning from implementation we are separating thinking from doing, and responsibility is diffused.

Francisco Pizarro coordinated strategy with tactics when he conquered the empire of the Incas with four dozen horses and a few hundred men.

- **Strategy:** Establish a method of communication.
- **Tactics:** Francisco got hold of an interpreter—Felipillo.

- **Strategy:** Communicate effectively.
- **Tactics:** Through Felipillo, the Spaniards cooed winning speeches to the Indians.

- **Strategy:** Implement activities to support your communication.
- **Tactics:** Trinkets were exchanged for gold and food. Smiles were the order of the day. To his men, Pizarro ordered, "Touch nothing, respect the inhabitants."

- **Strategy:** Play off one tribe against the other and fuel a civil war between the chiefs.
- **Tactics:** Attack the Incas' enemies (so they won't think you are the enemy).

- **Strategy:** Select the place and time for the decisive battle.
- **Tactics:** The Incas' "Waterloo" was the battle of Cajamarca.

Some claim it was the horse that conquered Peru. The Indians were confronted by well-armed men on horses—animals they had never seen before. How interesting it is that good fortune always seems to come to those who coordinate their strategic planning with tactical implementation.

Take the Offensive

The possibility of victory lies in the attack.
Generally, he who occupies the field of battle first
and awaits his enemy is at ease.

—Sun Tzu

Keys to a successful offensive are information, preparation, and skill. Often, the norm is the confusion of not enough information, not enough time to prepare, and not enough skills training.

Initiate Action

The most effective and decisive way to reach the objective is to seize, retain, and exploit the initiative. Being on the offensive puts you in control, and forces the foe to react rather than to act. An ancient proverb proclaims that "the first blow is as much as two."

Only by acting on the offensive in achieving your goal can you preserve freedom of action. Get too far behind and many of your actions must be a reaction to the leader. Get out in front and you are the leader.

In any offensive, mental action precedes physical action. Consequently, the offensive is often a great mental leap in the dark made at gut level. There are two mental approaches to launching an offensive:

1. *Plan everything in detail and then get going.* Too often, preparation is an excuse for procrastination. Although preparation should not be neglected, decisive action should not be delayed.

2. *Determine general objectives and then get going.* Details can be filled in as your offensive gains momentum.

It would seem that the choice is either to get ready or get going. Your greatest odds for success lie on the side of action.

I recall the dean of a prestigious law school telling me that in law school, you are trained to look at both sides of the situation and that is not good training for business. His observation is that people are better off deciding to do something rather than spending a lot of time analyzing the situation.

Keep on the Move

Inactivity causes more loss of opportunity than mistakes in the choice of methodology. Generals say:

If you want to determine the shape of the situation, fight and find out.

The offensive originates in our mind and then moves on to become a physical act. When I've been in the office for a week, I've generated enough activity to keep me in the office for another week. Similarly, when I've been in the field for a week, I've generated enough activity to keep me in the field for another week. However, there is a dramatic difference between the useful productivity of results from office-generated initiatives and field-generated initiatives.

I saw this problem when working at the corporate headquarters of a Fortune 500 company. The president, who spent weeks in the office managing from his desk, made decisions based on his historical experience. On the few occasions when the president did physically visit our customers, he would return to the office with new ideas. Unfortunately, the new actions were often misguided because they were based on conversations with a few customers in the same market.

Develop Spirit of the Offensive

An offensive spirit must permeate everything you do.

I've seldom found opportunity calling on me; instead, I've found opportunity outside the office. Even more important is the fact that being on the offensive visiting my market provides me with the timely information that keeps me on the cutting edge. When I've waited for information to be filtered through the bureaucracy, the offensive has been launched too late.

Schedule face time with people who are on the route you must travel to reach your goals. That helps put you in position to be master of the situation. Decisions about what to do become a matter of course when you spend time "where the action is."

Consider Alternative Routes

Sun Tzu says,

The army must know the five different attack situations and wait for appropriate times.

Here are a few different ways to take the initiative:

- *Launch a head-on attack.* This is often not the best route to your goal. It works only if you have overwhelming strength.
- *Use an indirect approach.* Instead of telling someone what to do, present facts, ask questions, and let the other person suggest a solution. That is, you help him or her think the solution is their idea.

  Taking a different type of indirect approach, fund-raising organizations will schedule events to raise money instead of asking for donations.
- *Be a guerrilla.* The guerrilla warrior carefully selects a point of attack where he can have an advantage. Guerrillas win with a series of minor coups that tip the scales.

Heed Rules for a Successful Offensive

Here are a few basic rules that will help you keep on the offensive:

1. *Be Professional:* In his book, *The Exceptional Executive,* Levinson identified the importance of knowledge to a professional:

   A professional is a person who can understand and apply scientific knowledge. Given knowledge, the professional can choose a course of action; he remains in charge of himself and his work.

   Knowledge is critical. The heartbeat of success is your knowledge in your area of expertise.

2. *Circulate to Percolate:* Network often and with people with different interests.

3. *Be Disciplined:* Plan your work and work your plan.

4. *Be a Difference Maker:* In sports, difference makers are players who cause good things to happen. Focus on making a positive difference.

5. *Keep on the Leading Edge:* Use the newest technology. For example, a digital video camera is a neat tool for showing visual images that excite people.

6. *Extend Every Contact:* A handwritten thank-you note is the extra step that shows appreciation and gets attention. Follow up with copies of articles that will interest the other person.

7. *Be Action-Oriented:* Keep things going by developing ongoing action plans. Involve others in your planning process.

In Summary

Take the initiative of action.
Develop an offensive spirit.
Keep on the move.

Move Rapidly

Speed is of the essence in war.
What is valued in war is a quick victory,
not prolonged operations.

—Sun Tzu

Speed is of the essence in war and winning.

Get Started

All of the positive consequences of speed accrue to the early offensive. The less you delay:

- The less apt you are to be surprised.
- The less ready will be your opponent.
- The greater the opportunity for surprise.

General Patton declared that a partially developed plan violently executed is superior to being late with a perfect plan. Too often, what impedes our progress is a lack of urgency. The problem is not just doing "it" rapidly, but rather deciding to do "it" at all.

Will Rogers said,

Even if your are on the right track, you'll get run over if you just sit there.

While we are procrastinating with our decisions, someone else is getting going. Although it is important to examine the problem and potential solutions before proceeding, beware of paralysis by analysis. Napoleon said that two-thirds of the decision-making process is based on analysis of information and one-third is a leap in the dark.

Although more data may be desirable—we never have enough data and neither does our opponent. Winners get going and fight their way through to the finish. Losers continue their search for the always elusive "more."

Time is the enemy. That is why many decisions must be made at gut level. Not making a decision is a decision. Not charting a course is a decision. In our lives, opportunities appear and disappear—in careers, in relationships, and in every thing we do.

When you know that Napoleon's troops marched at a rate of 120 paces per minute while his opponents marched at the more orthodox 70 paces, you know a fundamental advantage that contributed to his success. Think of the advantages that accrue if you are able to reduce by 50 percent the time required in initiating action.

Achieving the initiative by moving rapidly has a positive effect on morale. An ancient writer explains the morale factor this way:

Attack inspires the soldier . . . and confuses the enemy. The side under attack always overestimates the strength of the attacker.

The speed of the Mongol hordes invariably gave them a superiority of force at the decisive point, the ultimate aim of all tactics. By seizing the initiative and exploiting their mobility to the utmost, Mongol commanders were almost always able to select the point of decision.

Solve Differences Rapidly

The concept of rapid movement also applies to personal disagreements. It's important to get started solving the problem. The odds for mental well-being in any altercation lie on the side of getting through the difference. Sun Tzu advises,

> *While we have heard of stupid haste in war, we have not yet seen a clever operation that was prolonged. There has never been a case in which a prolonged war has benefited a country.*

The historic feud between the Hatfields and the McCoys is a classic example of carrying an altercation to the extreme. Every disagreement has two dimensions: time and depth. The longer the disagreement, the deeper the resulting emotional depth. Hatred grows over time. A common statement in arguments is "the more I thought about it, the madder I got." The advice is always, "get over it and go on with your life."

In Summary

Set timetables for action.
Develop a sense of urgency.
Get going and get done with it.

Gain Momentum

When torrential water tosses boulders,
it is because of momentum.

The energy is similar to a fully drawn crossbow.

The momentum of one skilled in war is overwhelming.
—Sun Tzu

Success requires not only the initial speed of the attack, but also a continuation of the initiative—it's called momentum.

Offensive action must be a continuing process. When you have momentum, you also have freedom of action—the opportunity to make the right decisions for the long term.

Here are key components of momentum:

- *One may feel protected from falling only when one is rising.* It's not difficult to understand that any positive action or degree of success generates positive emotions. Clausewitz says the pursuit is as important as the attack. Keep on the move.
- *Rapid decision-making produces rapid execution.* The shorter the decision time, the sooner a decision can be communicated. This allows everything to proceed more rapidly and leads to a greater probability of success. In contrast, delayed decisions inevitably lose their positive quality.

When you wait too long, your opponents have had time to prepare and your friends have lost patience.

- *Rapid action is simultaneous action.* When swiftness is at a maximum, it is easier to coordinate all actions into a simultaneous thrust.

In Summary

Decision time is the enemy.
Momentum preserves freedom of action.
Keeping on going is easier when on the move.

孫子

Take Advantage of Opportunities

A skilled commander sets great store
by using the situation to the best advantage.

—Sun Tzu

Success breeds success. Key to any successful equation is getting the first successful step and then leveraging additional success from each new victory.

Get Leverage

The first rule of good leveraging is that you must give leverage in order to get leverage. One-sided leverage produces the kind of pressure that destroys relationships. The person who gives no leverage gets none in return.

Airline frequent-flyer programs are examples of productive leverage. They succeed because they give the customer an opportunity to leverage his relationship. The more the airline gets what they want (the flier on their routes), the more benefits the flier accrues.

You can take advantage of leveraging opportunities in many of life's activities—for example, volunteer work in charitable organizations. The opportunities are endless, but your time resources are limited, so make choices that support personal objectives. David Thiel, founder of Auragen Communications, participates in charitable organizations to aid in pursuing political interests. Active membership in organizations like the United Way helps Thiel understand how the community works. By helping his community, he is leveraging his time to gain knowledge and contacts that can advance business and personal goals.

All you need to do to be a leader in these organizations is raise your hand and volunteer. Leaders give more to volunteer organizations and leaders get more from volunteer organizations in personal satisfaction and contacts that can be leveraged into other opportunities.

Wherever you have a relationship, your success can be leveraged. In sports, the team athlete knows that his success will be recognized by the coach and the greater the athlete's success, the greater his playing time in the game.

Advancement in your career is all about leverage. Going to the right school gives you leverage for getting your first job. Getting hired by the right company, gives you leverage for applying for a position with another company. Getting promoted gives you leverage within the company and in the job market.

One component of every decision concerning your career should be "does this move give me leverage?" Staying with a company and getting promoted can be great. However, at some point you may want to look for a new position.

A respected college professor advised that we should have five different jobs in the first five years—and be fired from one of them. Good advice? Perhaps. Let's dissect his overstatement:

1. *Five different jobs in the first five years:* The advice is to get different experiences with different companies. Moving around that much may not be a good idea, but looking is a good idea. A few years out of college, I found myself in a position where the seniority of peers hampered opportunities for advancement. The professor's advice encouraged me to look for another job. I found a better one very soon.

2. *Be fired from one:* Horrors! Why would anyone want to be fired? The point here is that you should be willing to be

aggressive enough to put your job at risk. On select occasions, we need to make a decision that can result in a big win. Success requires calculated risks.

Being successful without building a broad base can make you vulnerable in your career. The answer is to get the right kind of leverage.

When you get the new position, think carefully about what you are going to do the first day and the first week. The impression you make establishes your base for leverage. The most important activity may not be taking action, it may be attentive listening as you meet your new coworkers.

When the new director of a hospital stood at the employee entrance on the first day of his employment to meet everyone and shake their hand, he established the first link in communications. Having a video camera running during this welcoming event provided a method for learning names and faces. This simple action signaled the beginning of building the new relationships he needed to leverage his leadership position.

Leverage is a device for successful communications. It's getting the person you are trying to convince to agree on minor issues and pyramiding that agreement into acceptance of a major issue.

Develop an Opportunity List

A friend who went into business with a partner said that after losing a sale, his partner commented on the action necessary to succeed:

The opportunities we lose are often due to circumstances beyond our control like loss of funding or the buyer changing jobs. It seems that we need ten sure things for one to work.

Ever since then, I've developed a list of "ten sure things." Sometimes, I do not have ten prospective opportunities on my list. However, the search for additional opportunities to add to my list keeps me on the offensive. This keeps me from being discouraged when something doesn't work out. I know that I have other alternatives and simply go on to the next opportunity on my list. At the same time, I search for a new one to replace the one I lost.

Do It Now

Timing is of great importance in taking advantage of opportunities. The problem often is not that the time span is of a really short duration such as days or hours. It's things that can be done either this year or next that never get done.

Once again, the solution is a lifelong goal and timetable for accomplishment.

In Summary

Achieve the first success.
Then leverage to the next level.
Use leverage at every opportunity.

Be Persistent

Pursue one's own strategic designs to overawe the enemy.
Then one can take the enemy's cities
and overthrow the state.

—Sun Tzu

After deciding on a course of action, stick to it. This gives your plan the strength of consistency of action.

Determine an Implementation Methodology

You can roll out your plan sequentially, cumulatively, or simultaneously.

Sequential Implementation: A sequential approach to any project is a series of reinforcing steps. Success at each level sets the stage for moving to the next level.

General MacArthur's island-hopping drive up the Pacific is an example of the execution of a sequential operation.

A sequential job hunt would be to send out a resume and wait for a response before sending out the next one, obviously not a good idea in most instances. In contrast, your career path is a series of sequential steps, each making the next one possible.

Cumulative Implementation: A cumulative approach to any project is a multi-pronged approach with unconnected or dissimilar activities that eventually reach a critical mass.

The American submarine force attack in the Pacific is an example of a series of unrelated events accumulating the planned effect.

An exercise program involving diet and several exercise regimes is a cumulative approach to better physical well-being.

A cumulative job search would be characterized by taking a series of actions over a period of time such as, inquiries at a trade show, sending out resumes, checking with friends and calling headhunters. This is the type of activity where you "test the waters" to see what's available.

Simultaneous Implementation: This is a mass attack where a concentrated effort is launched across a wide front in a limited time span.

The German blitzkrieg across the Low Countries during World War II is an example of a simultaneous effort.

Any project where you concentrate multiple contacts in a short time is a blitz. For example, you could launch a phone blitz to get job interviews. Direct mail and phone blitzes are common actions by politicians just prior to election day.

What Counts Is Persistence

Admiral Rickover found that getting the backing for a nuclear submarine was almost as difficult as designing and building it. Rickover reminds us that:

> *Good ideas are not adopted automatically. They must be driven into practice with courageous patience.*

Sports coaches state simply, "When you are knocked down, get up!" Moreover, if your ideas fall flat, get up! If you are dead wrong, get up! Your personal mission is to storm the next barricade.

All implementation is goal-oriented. It's important to select the implementation process that works. For example, an athlete training for an event would probably succeed best with sequential implementation—

that is step-by-step improvement. A manager trying to build a stronger organization might find that a cumulative approach works best—that is, continually looking for good people. However, if he or she needed to move rapidly to fill positions, a blitz might be the right ticket to success.

In Summary

Sequential implementation requires step-by-step persistence.
Cumulative implementation requires random persistence.
Simultaneous implementation requires short-term
persistence over a wide front.

Occupy the High Ground

*In battle and maneuvering,
all armies prefer high ground to low ground.*
—Sun Tzu

Some 2,000 years later than Sun Tzu, Frederick the Great said:

The first rule that I give is always to occupy the heights.

The real question is not whether occupying the high ground is a good idea, but rather: "What is the high ground?"

In any endeavor, the high ground is both mental and physical. Improvements in either the mental or physical position are mutually supportive. For example, more security in the physical high ground makes for a healthier mental high ground. In turn, sound mental health leads to activities that build physical health.

Establish a Mental High Ground

The foundation of your mental high ground is in areas such as moral beliefs, personal integrity, and motivation towards success.

Moral beliefs: Most of all, the mental high ground is a moral position. It is where we have a belief "in the right" of our position. We have discussed moral strength earlier and recognized how emotional inputs can strengthen or destroy moral outputs. The battle for the moral high ground is waged in our minds and the minds of our opponents. Much of life is a battle of the mind because the best entries to the mind are often through emotions. Logic can sound great to the persuader, but emotions play a powerful role in determining courses of action.

Personal integrity: Here is another view of this personal quality we discussed earlier. I recall a young man telling me how easy it was to develop successful business relationships with customers. He said, "All you need to do is to tell them the truth." Good idea! The problem is that truths are elusive. What might be recognized as a truth on one day can be dispelled as a myth on another. Look at the constantly evolving world of medical advice as proof. Regarding certain treatments, medical doctors are often heard to say, "We don't do that any more." Truths change. Facts can be quicksand.

The wise man said long ago that "all generalizations are false, including this one." Certainly, one way to avoid making a statement that could later be proven inaccurate is not to make any statements. Obviously, this approach is a non-solution.

It's okay to take a position, but be open-minded. Finding "the best" is a continuous search.

Motivation: How many times have we heard "if you do not know where you are going, any road will take you there." Often, the problem with lack of direction is lack of motivation. When we are going nowhere, we are obviously in no hurry to get there.

Management expert Peter Drucker addresses the issue of knowing where you are going and getting there when he says,

Whenever anything is being accomplished, it is being done, I have learned, by a monomaniac with a mission. YEP!

Maxwell Maltz examined motivation and goal-orientation in his classic book, *Psychocybernetics*. The word "cyber" is derived from the Greek word for "steersman." Since "psycho" deals with the mind, psychocybernetics considers "steering the mind" or mental directions.

In his work in plastic surgery, Maltz discovered that some people who had reconstructive surgery were changed and others were not. For example, some who had a facial scar removed had a new self-image; others did not.

Maltz determined that the way we perceive our present and future has a great effect on how we act. People who are goal-oriented and moving towards that goal have more stability just as the person who is on a bicycle achieves stability by pedaling—and has none while standing still.

To state it simply: to keep going towards a goal is more important than reaching the goal. That is, being motivated towards success is what keeps us successful. Goal-directed actions produce dramatic results.

There are mountains of materials available to help us get better. A fast reader, who could read a book a day on self-improvement, could not read them all in a lifetime.

When interviewing people for new positions, I often ask the question, "What are the last five books you have read?" This unusual question often produces a chuckle and a variety of responses ranging from a comprehensive list of books to "I only read magazines." The answer gives me a snapshot of the interests of that person. What I'm looking for is that one of the books is on some topic that indicates a thirst for self-improvement. The books can be focused on improvement of any aspect of the personal or professional life. I want to employ someone focused on getting better and one way that can be measured is by knowing the candidate's reading preferences.

When interviewing salespeople, I always ask the question, "How did you learn how to sell?" One candidate replied, "Mr. Michaelson, I'm a natural-born salesman." Baloney! I believe that we are all "natural-born" and everything else is learned. I want to work with people who are willing to learn how to get better.

Secure Physical High Ground

The battle for the high ground in life is more mental than physical. However, without being able to actually see ourselves progressing toward, or reaching, the high ground, we lose confidence in our compass.

Position strength: In all of our families (nuclear, religious, career, and other interests), the position we hold identifies where we are on our climb to the high ground. Position is a source of identity and reward. The process of continually improving our position gives us stability in the uneven terrain of life.

Career security: Career paths can be crowded and disrupted by outside events over which we have no control.

A friend who had his company acquired by a new conglomerate sought a new position and received an excellent job offer which he accepted.

In counseling him on the move, I suggested that he not burn any bridges and that corporate exit interviewers should be considered a potential future employer. He later reported that the day after his exit interview with a senior manager, he received a phone call from another division asking him to come for an interview. Following advice, he politely declined stating that he had already accepted an offer. (To do otherwise would undermine his integrity.) He further indicated that he could consider offers only after spending time in his new position—a way of stating his loyalty and leaving an opening for opportunity.

By carefully orchestrating his exit, he strengthened his career security. The new job will give him new experience that will make him more valuable to any employer, including his old company. He is in the proverbial catbird seat for a while—he has a great new job and potential future opportunities with his previous employer. The path to the high ground is paved with stepping stones that we carefully place in position.

Physical health and fitness: Good mental health is a byproduct of being on the mental and physical high ground. Following advice on achieving the mental high ground does not assure physical health and fitness. A sound body is a product of physical conditioning.

Nothing epitomizes physical fitness more than a gold-medal winner in the Olympics. The names and feats are legendary. The focus of training for sports victories has moved from training harder to training smarter.

Sport-specific training doesn't mean performing the exact event. It does involve working the right muscles and training in the right pattern of movement to stimulate the neuromuscular systems needed to excel.

Bobsled racers practice sprinting in a shuffling style to learn how to impart take-off speed by keeping their feet on the ice. In contrast, a track sprinter's ideal practice attempts to keep feet in the air much of the time. Cross-country skiers work on upper body strength because scientists have found that upper body muscles are important in propelling racers forward rapidly. Luge racers work on torso strength and control as well as balance.

Winners in the high ground of life are in good mental and physical condition. The primary ingredient of a good exercise program is discipline. Get a schedule and then find the right types of exercise that work for you and your body.

In Summary

Head for the mental and physical high ground.
It takes a plan and discipline.
Start your engines.

Build on Your Success

To win battles and capture lands and cities,
but to fail to consolidate these achievements
is ominous
and may be described as
a waste of time and resources.

—Sun Tzu

The master is talking about a win that breeds the conditions that cause a loss. This is another case of "we have met the enemy and they are us."

Why is it that 95 percent of the people who lose weight gain it all back—and often more? Is it because they accepted the challenge and won—and then in winning they became complacent and lost?

In every task, we must project our vision tape to the end. That is, what do we want to accomplish long term? How do we transition from success in the short term to success in the long term?

We see the failure to pyramid success in sports teams who vanquish a very tough opponent. The exhilaration and sense of relief at winning the tough victory seems to temporarily dull the fighting edge. The loss of the strong drive to win often means the next game involves defeat by a less able opponent.

It is a military maxim that:

The greatest cause of defeat is victory.

The more successful we get, the more we tend to stop doing the things that made us successful. The deterioration of our own efforts opens the door to motivated opponents.

Business acquisitions can be a victory that leads to defeat because the different cultures fail to mesh. If you have ever been in a company that is being acquired, you have seen and felt the effects of internal clashes.

International economists talk about "the curse of resources." For examples, they point to countries such as:

- Argentina, which was a rich nation a century ago, thanks to its abundance of cattle and beef production. That prosperity bred a social-welfare system that eventually brought it to financial ruin.
- The oil-rich states of the Middle East have never weaned themselves from the dependence on oil income.

We see a similar decline caused by "the curse of resources" in the later generations of wealthy families.

A sad example of not taking advantage of victory is the person who gets a great education and then fails to use that knowledge base to leverage success.

Using Sun Tzu's words, our "consolidating of achievements" is taking inventory of our personal strengths and resources and determining how we can use these "weapons" to achieve the next level.

If this "consolidation of achievements" is only a mental exercise, chances are we will not move on. By putting a plan of action in writing, we take the first step on the road to success.

In Summary

You are a valuable resource.
Consolidate your achievements.
Success is a springboard to the next level.

Section Four
Competitive Success

Introduction

Get Your Priorities Right

Setting priorities is an essential element of every competitive engagement. Sun Tzu gives great advice:

1. *The best policy in war is to attack the enemy's strategy.*

   Attacking strategy means to "win without fighting." This is a mental battle that seeks to win through psychology. For example, "kill 'em with kindness" or achieve a level of excellence that discourages opposition.
2. *The second best way is to disrupt his alliances through diplomatic means.*

   "Diplomatic means" is, of course, negotiations. For example, "let's sit down and talk."
3. *The next best method is to attack his army in the field.*

   Attacking the army in the field would involve battle strategies like an indirect approach or blitz. This could be finding leverage or action that forces the issue in your favor.
4. *The worst policy is to attack walled cities. Attacking cities is the last resort when there is no alternative.*

   This is definitely a head-on attack. In life, it could be "taking the case to court," or expending a lot of resources to try to win.

It's clear that winning with strategy is better than winning by fighting—attaining competitive success does not always require conflict.

Pick Your Battles Carefully

If you are not sure of success, do not use troops.
If you are not in danger, do not fight.

—Sun Tzu

Sun Tzu's math lesson for determining odds of success is quite simple:

When ten to the enemy's one, surround him.
When five times his strength, attack him.
If double his strength, engage him.
If equally matched, be capable of dividing him.
If less in number, be capable of defending yourself.
And, if in all respects unequal, be capable of eluding him.
A weak force will eventually fall captive to a strong one if it
* simply holds ground and conducts a desperate defense.*

When Allied forces staged an invasion in America's island-hopping campaign in the Pacific, they tried to achieve a minimum of three-to-one superiority when their forces staged an invasion. If the Allied forces had invaded Japan, the planned strength was one-to-one. The Atom Bomb made the invasion unnecessary.

In today's world, technological strength can be more important than numerical strength. The important issue is that overwhelming strength succeeds. If not, you may be better served to look elsewhere for better odds for victory.

Avoid Political Battles

In Sun Tzu's ancient time, another Chinese warlord wrote:

> To *win victory is easy, to preserve its fruits, difficult. And there-*
> *fore it is said that when all under heaven is at war:*
> *One who gains one victory becomes the Emperor;*
> *One who gains two, a King;*
> *One who gains three, Lord Protector;*
> *One who gains four is exhausted;*
> *One who gains five victories suffers calamity.*
> *Thus, he who by countless victories has gained empire is unique,*
> *while those who have perished thereby are many.*

This quotation offers a special warning for political battles in the office or other activities. Don't fight if you do not have to fight. The danger is winning too many battles and making too many jealous enemies.

Know How to Win

Sun Tzu states a list of simple points that assure victory. Analysis after any battle reveals a few simple basic reasons why losers lost. The problem is not knowing why battles are lost; the problem is being smart enough to do the correct analysis prior to the event. Sun Tzu offers a simple plan for analysis that applies today.

> *There are five points in which victory may be predicted:*
> 1. *He who knows when to fight and when not to fight.*
>   Control your temper. Approach problems clinically.
> 2. *He who understands how to handle both superior and*
>   *inferior forces.*
>   Superior forces win; inferior forces lose unless they can
>   achieve a relative superiority.

3. *He whose ranks are united in purpose.*
   Believe in what you are doing.
4. *He who is well prepared and lies in wait for an enemy who is not well prepared.*
   Do your homework.
5. *He whose generals are able and not interfered with by the sovereign.*
   Think Vietnam, where President Johnson picked bombing targets.

Following these simple rules for winning will keep you on the road to success.

In Summary

Don't fight battles you cannot win.
Get the overwhelming odds on your side.
Winning too often in office politics can invite calamity.

Know Your Opponent

He who is not sage cannot use spies.
—Sun Tzu

Again, Sun Tzu says,

When you know yourself but not the enemy, your chances of winning and losing are equal.

Do the math. According to Sun Tzu's statement, equal chances of winning and losing means your chances of winning are reduced by half if you do not know your enemy.

Sun Tzu devotes his entire Chapter Thirteen to the employment of secret agents. The type of "spying" most of us might do today is quite different from that envisioned by Sun Tzu.

Sports coaches do not spy by sneaking in to watch a competitive team practice, rather they spy by purchasing film of the competitor playing a public game and seriously study play action. Using this information, the coach develops offensive and defensive plans and sets up a practice session against a team modeled after the opponents system. Is this an effective way of spying and using the information secured? Just ask any winning coach with an extensive library of films of opposing teams.

Build a Creative Information System

Every successful competitive endeavor, whether in business, sports, or politics, requires a flow of incoming information. Here are key steps in building that system.

Cultivate your contacts: With your own informal, organized information flow, you gain advantages in both time and accuracy. Close personal contact guards against filtered reports.

Responses to your inquiries must be nurtured with a message of appreciation to keep the information flowing. Contact information systems work only when the outgoing flow matches the incoming flow.

Snapshots build pictures: Our world of available information is vastly expanded by contacts on the Internet. For example, when I wanted to find out business conditions in another industry, I e-mailed a contact made playing golf in Hawaii. His reply gave me a snapshot of the current situation in another city. Other contacts gave me a series of snapshots to get the big picture.

When a retailer told me his business was unusually slow, I sought other snapshots in order to build my own financial picture of an impending downturn. This encouraged me to adjust my stock portfolio. When the adjustment turned out to be the right decision, I kept in touch with my sources because their information would be valuable for future decisions.

Validate your sources. Although number of contacts is important, seek to validate who is the best of your information cadre. Some will simply provide data while others will provide analysis and insights that are of great value. As you work the system, you will determine which sources are the most reliable and provide the best insights. Cultivate and nurture these relationships. This is where the gold is buried.

Put it all together: First, you must develop a network. Then you must evaluate the usefulness of information from your sources. Finally, you must cultivate the best of your network. Only then, will you have an information system that aids in your solutions.

Identify the Enemy

The enemy is anyone with the power to keep you from winning. Be sure to clearly define who is and who is not "the enemy." To the business person, the enemy is the competitor. In sports, it is the opponent. To the teacher, it may be some blocker in the educational process. In many situations, the enemy will be the system and not the people who must work within the system.

The enemy is never a close friend or marriage partner. The mental set of viewing someone who can be an ally as an enemy leads to actions that destroy the relationship.

The struggle with ourselves as the enemy often requires overcoming some personal weakness or lack of confidence. We need a close relationship with personal gurus and coaches to overcome these weaknesses. How often have we seen people held back, not by lack of ability, but rather by a lack of confidence in their ability to grow.

Understand Style

Frederick the Great said:

A great advantage is drawn from the knowledge of your adversary, and when you know his intelligence and character you can use it to play to his weakness.

Learning about your opponent involves both knowing what he or she is doing now and what he or she has done in the past. Go beyond the issues to look at personalities. Analyze the situation in terms of its history—who did something like this before and what happened. Look at the personalities in terms of their background of experience—where did they acquire their expertise and what have they done in similar situations.

For example, if you want to know the style of a new employee, supervisor, preacher, or club officer, look at the style where they were previously. All new arrivals bring their personal strengths and weaknesses with them. Each will tend to clone the style of his or her previous organization. When a new leader introduces change, that person is merely introducing the system with which he or she is comfortable. Accept the change and rally around the new leader.

In Summary

Identify the opposition.
Understand his or her style.
Make sure you are not the enemy.

Skillful Attacks Win

Take advantage of the enemy's unpreparedness,
make your way by unexpected routes,
attack where he has taken no precautions.

Against those skillful in attack,
the enemy does not know where to defend.

—Sun Tzu

Several issues are common to any skillful attack:

1. *A focal point*: Concentrate a critical mass.
2. *Surprise*: Be unpredictable.
3. *Follow through:* When it works, keep on using it.

Concentrate on a Focal Point

The first action decision is what are you going to do—that is, what is your plan and where should you focus the critical mass of resources?

- *A plan:* Put yourself in your opponent's shoes. How would he organize an attack? Use this analysis to organize your own attack.

   One of the most productive exercises in seminars I conduct is to ask participants to imagine they are now employed by their strongest competitor. Teams are asked to identify the strategies and tactics required for this competitor to win. Learning what their competitor would do yields valuable insight into their own plan of attack. The exercise also reveals where they are most vulnerable.

- *A critical mass:* When you have decided that the objective is worth winning, then you must allocate resources. It takes keen insight to determine the critical mass. A fog often masks what is really happening. Of all the things that need to be done to achieve success, many are good ideas, some are important, but only a few are critical.

A U.S. Army Chief of Staff for Plans and Preparations described the allocation of resources this way:

The efficient commander does not seek to use just enough means, but an excess of means.

A military force that is just strong enough to take an objective will suffer heavy casualties; a force vastly superior to the enemy's will do the job without serious loss of men.
—General Mark S. Watson, 1950

The above quote can simply be restated: to be sure of winning you must apply more than enough resources. Attacks with overwhelming superiority suffer relatively few casualties. The greater the strength of your attack, the less likely you are to be beat up in the process. Of course, the reference to "strength of your attack" applies to all facets of strength: moral, mental, and physical. The concept of applying overwhelming strength applies to any attack whether it is against an opponent or for a personal objective—such as a career position.

Sun Tzu states the power this way:

An army superior in strength takes action like the bursting of pent-up waters into a chasm of a thousand fathoms deep. This is what the disposition of military strength means in the actions of war.

Plan Surprise

You are most vulnerable to attack when standing still. Keep moving towards your objective.

In 1747, Frederick the Great advised his generals:

Everything which the enemy least expects will succeed the best.

A sound principle of management is that the manager should be predictable so that his or her people can take action without asking for authority.

In contrast, in competitive situations the attack that is least predictable is the one most likely to succeed. You see this often in sports. It's the quarterback sneak or the fake pass in football. Instead of kicking a field goal, it's running or passing the ball for two points.

To achieve surprise it is not necessary that your opponent be taken completely unaware; it is only important that he becomes aware too late to react effectively.

Carl von Clausewitz writes,

Surprise achieves superiority almost as strongly as direct concentration of forces.

A report in *Newsweek* about the war in Afghanistan stated, ". . . as the Americans withdrew. A Taliban commander ordered his tanks to open fire but U.S. bombs destroyed them first. An observer commented, "What kind of an army are these Americans? It was amazing to see how they destroyed our tanks." Similarly, an Iraqi officer in the Gulf War said, "We didn't know the Americans were in the area until the turret blew off one of our tanks."

The best kind of surprise is when the opponent doesn't know that he or she has been surprised. The deed is done without the opponent aware of how it happened. You see this scenario most often in office politics.

Follow Through

Anyone who has ever learned how to throw a ball knows the importance of follow through. The continued forward motion of the arm after the ball leaves your hand is not a separate step, it's a component of the entire process.

Understand that your opponent has weaknesses and be prepared to exploit them. Keep on doing whatever works. However, doing the same thing that worked before will not work forever. Eventually, your opponent will figure out how to counter your action. Long before that happens is when you need to think about innovation.

In Summary

Focus.
Plan a surprise attack.
Keep on doing what works until innovation works better.

Timing Js Everything

When the strike of the hawk
breaks the body of its prey, it is because of timing.
The timing is similar to the release of the trigger.
—Sun Tzu

In achieving success, the role of timing has many components. Fast movement precedes "the strike of the hawk," great power is generated at the point of attack and, of course, all of this works best at the right moment.

Get Started

As a rule, earliest is best. Make a decision and get going.

The later you start, the more you require. The longer it takes to begin the action, the more speed will be required later.

If you wait for approval, you will be late. It is often better to seek forgiveness, than to ask permission.

Keep Ahead of Your Opponent

Among fighter pilots, "getting inside" an opponent requires maneuvering faster than your opponent. This increased agility allows you to get a good fix on your opponent.

"This mobility is key," says John Boyd, a retired fighter pilot and recognized expert on maneuvering. Boyd's key to success is generating

Use sparingly

a mismatch by getting inside your opponent's "observation-orientation-decision-action" time cycle. By the time your opponent "observes" what you are doing, "orients" his thinking to it, "decides" what to do and "acts," his response will be too late.

This competitive tactic, like many, is both physical and mental. Your mind is conditioned to generate the speed of physical actions that surprise and confuse your opponent. This places your adversary in the position of focusing his mind on what you are doing and reacting. In real life, the process of keeping ahead of your opponent can be a single action, but is most often a series of actions.

You see it in sports when teams are continually changing plays and presenting "different looks" to their opponents as they race to victory. You see it in competitive actions where innovation defeats an opponent mentally and physically.

Anytime you can preempt an opponent's action, you have a real possibility of generating a mismatch that works in your favor. A superior fighter doesn't just parry his adversary's thrust, he gets off one of his own as he operates within his opponent's ability to respond. Even if the opponent seems to have every advantage, a well-timed attack can uncover weakness.

Speed and movement are the first two essentials to this successful attack. They are key to generating the initial mismatch and beginning the cascading circumstances that keep you ahead of your opponent.

In Summary

Don't delay.
Generate the mismatch.
Use speed and maneuver to win.

Section Five
Examples of Success

Introduction

Apply the Wisdom

Way back at the beginning of time, two men wanted to test the wisdom of a country's oracle. They decided upon a plan. They would appear before the oracle with a bird in their hand with some of the feathers showing and would ask, "What is it I hold in my hand?'

Seeing the feathers, the oracle would respond, "It is a bird."

Then the men would ask, "Is the bird dead or alive?"

If the oracle said the bird was alive, they would crush their hand and let it fall to the floor dead. If he said it was dead, they would open their hand and let it fly away.

At the appointed time, they appeared before the oracle.

To the question, "What is it I hold in my hand?" the oracle responded, "It is a bird."

Then they asked, "Is it dead or alive?"

The oracle responded, "I do not know, you hold its future in your hand!"

Your future is your decision. The following examples illustrate how leading-edge thinkers and doers apply Sun Tzu's wisdom to enhance their future.

Coaching Challenges

Lou Sartori
History Teacher and Girls' Varsity Basketball Coach
Seneca High School, Louisville, KY

My first contact with *The Art of War* and Sun Tzu fell upon deaf ears. It was in the early 1980s when attending a basketball coaching clinic. I wanted to learn the x's and o's and become a successful teacher/coach. The speaker was Bobby Knight. He mentioned how Sun Tzu's book was full of philosophy and practical applications. Needless to say, I ignored the book upon this first encounter.

Several years later, after attending numerous other clinics and hearing the same description from time to time, I finally decided to purchase *The Art of War* and read it. My eyes were finally opened and I have tried to follow certain guidelines and principles ever since.

Sun Tzu undoubtedly was a master teacher and would have had many undefeated "teams." The themes that keep pounding at me from the book are many. They have helped me to mature and grow as a teacher/coach. Although I could go on, the themes of preparation, discipline, and communication are the major ones I have applied.

Preparation. As a teacher/coach today, I have many different roles that I must play. Sun Tzu's early warning "know your enemy and know yourself" (Chapter 3) teaches us that preparation and planning is vital. This precept encourages me to make plans—lesson plans for the classroom, and practice plans for the court. Many people, including colleagues, have been complimentary of my organizational skills. I owe it all to Sun Tzu who points out the calamities of not planning or being prepared. I believe that "failing to plan is planning to fail." Too many teachers today consider lesson plans a necessary evil, if they do them at all. Some schools require that lesson plans be turned in every week. Although our school has no such requirement, I draft a set every week. It keeps me on track.

Discipline. A proverbial problem for most teachers is classroom discipline. I recommend that teachers, coaches, and managers apply Sun Tzu's idea that soldiers must be treated with humanity but kept under control by iron discipline (Chapter 9). In 29 years of teaching and coaching I have had my share of problems, but they have been kept to a minimum. My teaching evaluations have stressed that a learning atmosphere exists in my classroom based upon firm, fair discipline.

Another principle from Sun Tzu affects how I discipline. He constantly stresses that orders (directions) must be clear and distinct. I've tried to use this technique throughout my career. Communication is very important in any endeavor and I have used the K-I-S-S (Keep It Simple Stupid) approach effectively in my role as a coach.

Communication. When I arrived at my present school, female students had very limited experience trying out for basketball. Effective, distinct communication was the biggest adjustment I had to make. It is critical to speak in a manner that your students comprehend. There is no need to show off your education and intelligence by using words that are not understood. You will immediately know if they "get it;" or, "don't get it." The blank, dazed looks speak volumes. My directions may seem very elementary; however, they have been followed completely for all assignments.

I owe a debt of gratitude to Sun Tzu. My career has been very rewarding. Teaching today's youth is very challenging; yet the task has been pleasant and the journey is one that I would not trade.

Winning Battles

Terri D. Nance
Vice President—Business Intelligence
Ingram Book Company

Sun Tzu advises to *fight only battles you can win.* This advice is very useful in making effective choices when dealing with conflicting initiatives.

As a young woman I was faced with a difficult choice, borrow extensively to attend college or work to support myself and go to school part-time at night.

Following Sun Tzu's advice to *make an assessment,* I determined that my best strategy would be to work during the day and go to school at night.

I was now focused on the goal and my ability to commit my resources. As Sun Tzu says, I had kicked the ladder away. The intensity made me much more focused.

By following Sun Tzu's advice to "fight only the battles I could win," I was able to accomplish much more than originally planned. I've gone on to complete a master's degree.

As I entered a career with a large corporation I found new applications for Sun Tzu. My intuition told me that the wisdom behind Sun Tzu's words would ultimately prove applicable in dealing with internal corporate politics and constraints. However, one cannot really afford to apply Sun Tzu's advice too literally when dealing with internal business associates. Using deception and employing spies would be suicidal to one's career, at least in most companies.

Two previous attempts to implement enterprise-wide project management ended in failure. My breakthrough in analyzing Sun Tzu's application to business came as an epiphany. Imagining the enemy as organizational obstacles helped me in my daunting task of building a project management system for a large information technology division.

The following key concepts were applied to remove organizational barriers.

> *Apply extraordinary force.* Despite the general resistance to another try at project management, I knew from my reconnaissance at the coffee machine that several managers were frustrated at the inability of the department to get projects completed on time and within budget. I recruited an *"extraordinary force"* to help slay the enemy of organizational malaise. These managers proved invaluable in overcoming the most fortified pockets of resistance.
>
> *Plan Surprise.* The little pilot project we started had no resistance in the hinterlands of the division we chose for this first small step. However, once the methodology proved both simple and robust, we asked the head of the division to present it as a mandated initiative at the next general staff meeting. We moved from a pilot to a full divisional mandate before naysayers could organize resistance.
>
> *Reinforce strength not weakness.* Once the surprise worked, we pursued a rollout. My initial inclination was to attack the most resistant departments first, but Sun Tzu's advice to reinforce strength not weakness turned my mind. Instead of attacking the bastions of negative thought, we identified the allies and the uncommitted. We kept a careful

accounting as department after department adopted the
new methodology.

Be flexible. Sun Tzu consistently emphasizes the need for flexibility in the face of changing circumstances. Allowing flexibility in the method but enforcing great discipline in the
output gave us a winning system. This approach proved
informative to the executive leadership, improved our
relationships with internal customers, and avoided sad-
dling managers with unnecessary bureaucracy.

Consider tactical options. Sun Tzu advises *there are some roads
which must not be taken . . . some cities which must not be
assaulted.* We had one such citadel in our division where
we decided to forego full-blown project management
implementation. We simply asked this group to provide
estimates of the project hours on each of their major projects. This accomplished about 80 percent of the goal
without having to lay siege to the manager.

Consolidate your gains. As we made progress with our project
management methodology, we began to see real gains in
our performance and our relationships with the business
units we supported. Regular updates made it easy for the
leadership to see where their projects stood in the overall
scheme. As satisfaction grew, we were able to trumpet our
successes and build better relationships. Some of the
naysayers became strong allies and acknowledged that the
methodolgy was "working better than I thought it would."

   The wisdom of Sun Tzu is easily employed in a noncombative situation. Whether the enemy is a virus or failing public schools or
tobacco use among teenagers, it is not necessary to attack the people—
one can attack the problem quite successfully with a two-thousand-
year-old military strategy.

Leadership Lessons

Mark Davidoff
Executive Director and COO
Jewish Federation of Metropolitan Detroit

What is leadership? Leadership is the art of communicating vision. It is about the design of strategy. It is the establishment of objectives and marshaling of resources to realize these objectives. Leadership is about making difficult decisions that impact the lives of those you serve and those with whom you serve.

In Sun Tzu's writings, he delineates the common flaws of leadership as recklessness, cowardice, hasty temper, delicate honor, and over-solicitude. It is in the last of that he warns *those who love people can be troubled.* I have transformed this teaching into a basic rule of leadership that I am reminded of on a daily basis. Get your love at home.

Business leaders must make difficult decisions on a constant basis. In making decisions, leaders must always determine what is in the best interest of the "sovereign," as Sun Tzu would call today's stakeholders. Discipline "in the best interests of stakeholders" applies to all businesses, nonprofit service providers, and government agencies. Having held various leadership positions in nonprofit social welfare and health service organizations over the past 15 years, I have often been faced with deciding which service to fund, program to cut, segment of the populations is in greatest need, and employees no longer add value. Absent a clear mind, no such decisions could be made correctly.

Leaders who look to the work environment for their deepest friendships, glory, ego boosts, and love will not deliver. The leader who can control his or her "over-solicitude" and get his or her love at home will function with a clear mind and a solid heart.

Institutions are permanent fixtures on the landscape of our communities. The individuals who fill the offices of these institutions over time are no more than stewards for the next generation. As a community leader with this heavy responsibility, I approach each day with a deep breath and a steady pace, being mindful of the fatal flaws of leadership described by Sun Tzu.

Relevant Principles

Les Lunceford, (retired U.S. Marine Corps officer)
President, The Transition Team, Inc.
Knoxville Operations

I read *The Art of War* in college and several times as a Marine officer; its applicability to private enterprise came later in my life. Sun Tzu's treasure chest of knowledge made a significant difference in my military career and that of fellow officers. *The Art of War* makes a difference for anyone who takes the time to read, understand, and actively apply the strategies.

It is a major mistake to read Sun Tzu and walk away feeling merely enlightened. Enlightenment is of little value without wind in the sails provided by ACTION.

Victory on the battlefield or in business is seldom achieved with the application of a single principle. When it came time for me to transition into business, more than one of Sun Tzu's principles unlocked winning concepts and pushed me to exceed my greatest expectations. Sun Tzu's principles served as a force multiplier—a concept drilled into me and all other military officers. Force multipliers (using multiple principles) apply additional pressure on the competition and reinforce momentum. In particular, four principles have had an impact on our business's success:

Thoroughly assess conditions. Good assessment is the foundation of a successful operation. Before we developed a marketing plan, we had to thoroughly assess our competitors, the market area, our weaknesses, our strengths, and feedback from existing clients. We found 23 percent of our customers were providing 80 percent of our revenues. Had we not accomplished a thorough assessment, we were about to lean our ladder to success against the wrong wall.

We focused on better serving existing clients because the high cost of acquiring new customers depletes resources faster than the cost of satisfying existing ones. This produced record results. Preparing any plan without a thorough assessment is like building a house on shifting sands; the house won't survive.

People are a valuable asset. Sun Tzu says, "He treats them as his own beloved sons and they will stand by him until death." When we treat others with respect, dignity, and as we'd like to be treated, we're displaying a sincere regard for those we're entrusted to lead. Genuine regard for other people helps us produce desired results.

Do not read Sun Tzu thinking its primary purpose is to get more work out of people so you can have more success for yourself. The principles in *The Art of War* are about the power to support others and make differences in their lives. I am talking about the power that comes from personal conviction; the power to lead and the power to visualize the future. When you make positive differences in other people's lives, you will notice that the world relates differently to you.

Be Flexible. While strategies remain constant, tactics must be adapted to each new situation. Being successful in business or war requires simultaneous planning and action. While initial planning is important, too much planning can be disastrous. Any plan must be the basis for change. Plans must not be so rigid that adjustments can't be made as the situation changes.

Know Your Terrain. Know the needs of the customer, the strengths and weaknesses of your team and opponents. After the September 11 terrorist attacks, our clients' needs dramatically increased.

Following those tragic events, we further developed our executive coaching capabilities; established an executive search arm of our business; invested considerable capital and structure. We demonstrated to our customers that we understood their needs and stood ready to assist them.

"The Art of War"
Is the Art of Peace

Colin Benjamin
Managing Director, Intellectual Property Holdings
South Melbourne, Australia

The writings of Sun Tzu have consistently delivered practical wisdom in my personal search for a creative approach to personal conflicts and challenging opportunities. Sun Tzu continues to offer practical advice in my daily battles to balance business survival with the desire to undertake struggles for social justice around the world.

For more than 40 years I have studied *The Art of War* as a source of strategic guidance. This study included the works of Niccolo Machiavelli, De Jomini, and Mao Ze Dung as I attempted to identify the differences between the mind of the military and civilian strategists.

In this extensive study, the practical wisdom of Sun Tzu shines like a beacon—the battle is not the war. The war is won in the mind of the opposing forces, not on the battleground. Peace, not war, is the key to best practices in strategy.

The works of Rudyard Kipling, Ian Fleming, Le Carré, Arthur Conan Doyle, and Tolkien proved literary ammunition for an appreciation of the genius of Chapter Thirteen on "The Employment of Secret Agents." Here, in one short chapter, is a profound insight into the Art of Peace—the means of avoiding unnecessary loss of life with practical, down-to-earth instruction on the management of people in the world of spies and secrets.

As a student participant in organizing anti-conscription for Vietnam campaigns, while also serving as a member of the volunteer Citizens Military Forces, I was in a strategic double bind.

My service was as a member of a psychology corps responsible for officer selection. As a result, I was placed in charge of a psychological warfare resource designed to understand the mind of the enemy. This led me for the first time to Sun Tzu' s *The Art of War* and a lifetime interest in the mind of my opponent.

Australia entered the Vietnam War late in the campaign, much like it entered the war in Afghanistan. We adopted this position in support of the ANZUS alliance and in recognition of America's decisive role in defense against external aggression. My unit was in a psychology corps responsible for officer selection. As a clinician working in the field of mental health and clinical psychology, I was naturally interested in this field of study. I soon found the hidden genius in Sun Tzu. Here was a mother lode of wisdom, with passages such as "Therefore, the skillful leader subdues the enemy's troops without fighting," and "The supreme excellence is breaking the enemy's resistance without fighting."

Regular visits to China over the past 20 years have given me the chance to work with Chinese professors, entrepreneurs, and military leaders seeking to apply the thinking of Sun Tzu to the development of national enterprises. All have shared their view of Sun Tzu's work as a reference to the realities of commercial conflict with community goals. Sun Tzu's emphasis on winning with strategy is a counterpoint to the more action-oriented Western thinking.

It has been humbling to learn how to apply this ancient strategist's thinking to the construction of new community initiatives and government programs—all more than two centuries after *The Art of War* was written. Working for government ministers, multinational corporations, and my own firms offers a constant reminder of one of Sun Tzu's key rejoinders: "In battle, there are not more than two methods of attack—the direct and the indirect; yet these two in combination give rise to an endless series of maneuvers."

In summary, the struggle to apply Sun Tzu's wisdom has provided a valuable insight into the military and political mind. I see that every day it is necessary to survey the competitive terrain, identify the paths to success, and build a platform for achievement. The lessons learned are that peace is not just the absence of war. Peace is a measure of goodwill, personal trust, and freedom.

Rules for Daily Life

Benefsheh D. Shamley
Captain, U.S. Army
Commanding

As an Army officer and commander of troops, the concepts in Sun Tzu's *The Art of War* are very applicable to me. Study helped me realize how to apply the rules in my daily life.

"Know yourself; know your opponent" is my favorite rule. Knowing yourself can be tricky. I don't know how many times I've sat in front of superiors and they've told me to tell them my strengths and weaknesses. I usually just stare back for a while and sputter out something unintelligible. Why is this so hard? For me, I think it's because I really didn't want to know my weaknesses. We are always comparing ourselves to others and thinking "she's skinnier, prettier, smarter, and happier than I am." Yet, this serves no purpose and is self-defeating.

Instead of focusing on what others may think or how I measure up to someone else, I've learned to rely on my own assessment of myself. Today, I look at myself and address my weaknesses (as much as I hate to admit them) and concentrate on improving those that I can. It is important to be honest with yourself and to assess your strengths as well. This is half of the battle. When I know what I am capable of, with a little bit of research I can attack any situation (opponent) that may cross my path. This is a continuous process that I go through almost daily.

"Develop effective internal communications" is the next rule I use quite often. I have been lucky to have a very open and loving family. I talk to my parents frequently about various subjects and ask for advice. This strong bond is important in other life relationships. It goes without saying that it is important to communicate effectively with your superiors and subordinates at work. Simple problems get blown out of proportion because of miscommunication. Effective communication is also very important in dealing with friends and love relationships.

Several years ago, I had a very good friend with whom I failed to communicate. We were roommates for a few months and subtle things she did annoyed me. I never told her. Our relationship took a turn for the worse and one day I "blew up" and told her to move out. Afterwards, I regretted my actions and felt a tremendous amount of guilt. If I had told her what was bothering me as it occurred, we might still be friends today.

"Thoroughly assess conditions" and *"compare attributes"* are two principles I use in just about everything I do. These rules are key to major decisions such as buying a house or car, career choices, or planning a wedding. I assess the conditions of my situation using the five constant factors:

Moral influence: What impact will taking this assignment have on my family?
Weather: Are there outside circumstances to take into consideration?
Terrain: Where will this assignment take me?
Commander: What will be my job and for whom will I work?
Doctrine: Do I have the knowledge to qualify for the job, or do I need additional schooling?

Adjusting these five factors to my personal situation allows me to make a good assessment. I then compare the positive and negative attributes in order to make an informed decision. This simple process helps make sure I have looked at all options.

"Discipline can build allegiance" is another rule no one should live without. My inherent sense of self-discipline was enhanced by my time at West Point. Discipline allows a person to achieve his or her goals in academics, career, sports, or personal life. The hardest thing is telling myself what to do to succeed. Many times, especially now that I'm in command post, I tend to ignore my own disciplinary needs and focus on my soldiers. This is okay, as long as I don't neglect what I need to do to stay on track career-wise—physically and emotionally. It may take my fiancée, parents, or a friend to make me see where I need to be. It hurts to realize that you're not trying as hard as you can, or that you can be apathetic, but it happens to everyone. What you do to solve your problems depends on self-discipline.

Effective Decisions

Robert Jerus, Professor
Southeastern College

Sun Tzu says, *"The quality of decision is like the well-timed swoop of a falcon . . ."*

The distinguishing characteristic of effective people is their ability to implement high-quality decisions. Sun Tzu's concepts provide the tools for honing decision-making skills. The master strategist repeatedly refers to expertise in long- and short-term planning; information gathering, analysis, and action.

Sun Tzu indirectly points out that failure teaches. We need to learn from past performances. Lost battles have their place in winning the war.

Decision-making skills distinguish between people who really have a grasp on achievement and those who live in quiet disappointment. The final, critical component lies in the boldness to act. Most people have visions, develop ambitions, and make tentative plans for attainment, but fail to transform dreams into reality.

Dreams have their place. Life is hollow without aspirations and hopes for the future. Championships lie in the implementation of plans. Strategies and tactics provide the operational framework for winning. Success is in living.

There are always reasons to postpone actions. If life is spent waiting for the perfect opportunity and most advantageous time to capitalize on that opportunity, life will pass by with quiet regret. Those who wonder "what if" are doomed.

Consider Sun Tzu's falcon. The powerful swoop to capture prey is essential to survival. As a hunter, the falcon's sight and flight abilities are designed for action. The keen sight, speed, and patience culminate in success.

Quality decision-making followed by action is the core of Sun Tzu's teaching. Success in life, as on the battlefield, is the product of information, analysis, and critically, the decision to act.

Perhaps the most striking example of effective decision-making I have ever seen was when I met a most unusual college freshman. The gentleman, I'll call him Jack, explained that he intended to be President of the United States. I held back my laughter when I realized he was quite serious. He had decided to major in accounting noting that the President would have vast financial responsibility. In college, Jack was actively networking in the community because he deemed this activity critical to his mission.

After four years, he graduated very high in his program and continued on to law school. Within a few years, he earned his C.P.A. and graduated near the top of his class. Jack continued community service and joined a prominent law firm.

For a few years, I lost track of him. When I met him again, he was in his early thirties. At this point he owned a successful law firm and was married with two children. I asked him about his dream to become President. He thought I had forgotten as he responded with a wide grin and carefully explained the decision was the root of his success. By following Sun Tzu's advice, his powerful decision had given direction to his life and training—it generated opportunities. Jack advised me of the power of decisions, something I should have been telling him.

Sun Tzu teaches the value of decisions followed by action. When implementing your dreams, good things happen.

Implementing Strategy

Ivan Larsh
Former Captain, U.S.M.C.
Corporate President (Retired)

One would think that my education at the U.S. Naval Academy would have included the teachings of Sun Tzu. Since Sun Tzu had no Navy, perhaps this omission is understandable although I could have learned much about strategy from him. Oddly enough, not even my infantry training as a junior officer in the Marine Corps or flight training as a young fighter pilot included the study of Sun Tzu.

I first learned of the master from his most ardent advocate and interpreter, Gerald Michaelson, as he facilitated a strategic planning session for my company in 1998. The financial performance of the company had been strong compared to industry standards, but top-line growth was anemic. All strategic paths that diverged from our historical norm seemed littered with major hazards.

"Stick to your knitting" is a recurring theme of Tom Peters in his book *In Search of Excellence*, and was also the sentiment frequently voiced by the more conservative members of our management team.

"Identifying strengths." Michaelson's advice: listen to Sun Tzu. *"Now an army may be likened to water, for just as flowing water avoids the heights and hastens to the lowlands, so an army avoids strength and strikes weakness"* Simply stated, battles are won by concentrating strengths against weakness—always.

With Michaelson's urging, the team embraced a process for identifying our strengths that could be amassed to assure victory against the corresponding weaknesses of our competitors. This part of the process was invigorating! Team members were encouraged by their ability to reach consensus on several competitive advantages that we viewed as dominant and sustainable.

"Identifying weakness." Then came the hard part—being honest about our weaknesses and vulnerabilities to attack by competitors. Again, we listened to Sun Tzu. *"Invincibility lies in the defense, the possibility of victory in the attack. One defends when his strength is inadequate; he attacks when it is abundant."*

It had been more fun to talk about our abundant strengths; but we clearly had inadequacies. In business, as in battle, if you are not on offense, you are on defense. It seemed to us that the best way to defend our areas of weakness was to convert them to offensive actions. We brainstormed the various ways that we could mount guerrilla-like attacks from our weaker positions, capturing small footholds inside our competitor's circle of strength while avoiding major battles against a superior enemy.

We envisioned small outposts in foreign countries, strategic alliances with non-competing companies, ways to broaden our market position, lower cost positions and systems integration. Suddenly, playing defense seemed more fun!

From analysis to strategy. Finally, a strategy was emerging that assured steady generic growth from our strengths and also held the promise of additional growth from guerrilla-like offensive actions into new territories.

There are clearly two distinct activities in all strategic exercise: firstly, the planning and preparation; secondly, the conduct or execution. History (and personal experience) demonstrates that an average strategy, superbly executed, is more effective than a superb strategy with average execution. Sun Tzu has plenty to say about execution, but timing is one of the most important, *"Speed is the essence of war [or business]. Take advantage of the enemy's unpreparedness; travel by unexpected routes and strike him where he has taken no precautions."*

None of us will become great leaders simply by reading the words of great leaders. However, we can become substantially better managers, better planners, better at execution, by studying the expert teachings that have stood the test of time. Whether one is seeking victory on the battlefield, in the world of business, or in personal life, the teachings expressed by Sun Tzu in *The Art of War* more than 25 centuries ago are still remarkably current and beneficial.

Study the Principles

Edward Speed
Senior V.P., Strategic Planning
San Antonio Credit Union

When introduced to *The Art of War* as a young officer with the 3rd Armored Division, I was told that many people know about the book, but few understand it. Remembering that admonition, I rarely discuss the Master's works unless I know that the person with whom I am speaking has more than a casual familiarity with the content.

I was harshly reminded of this at a management conference when I mentioned the applicability of *The Art of War* to a particular business situation. A female management colleague loudly and derisively announced "there was no place in business today for war-like approaches taken from books awash in testosterone."

The appropriate response to arrogance laced with ignorance is always that of watchful quietude, so I remained silent.

What my very talented, yet young and unwise, associate did not understand is that *The Art of War* is anything but "war-like" and actually eschews aggression.

The Art of War is probably inappropriate reading for anyone without significant amounts of gray hair. To understand *The Art of War* and put its principles into practice one must be "docile" in the true, root-meaning of the word. Our word "docile" comes to us via French from the Latin adjective "docilis" meaning "easily taught." It later came to mean a willingness to be taught or a willingness to learn. Thus, a docile person is the student par-excellence, one who continually and willingly learns. Unfortunately, today the word docile is rarely used except as a pejorative.

It is openness to learning that is at the heart of *The Art of War:* continuous, insightful, honest observance and acceptance of the facts. It is seeing reality in its most raw form, not what one wishes reality to be.

This is overwhelmingly obvious to those of us who study and refer to Sun Tzu as we go about our business. In his opening statement, the Master says that war must be studied. He immediately states that one must appraise and compare. In listing the qualities of a general, Sun Tzu lists wisdom, sincerity, humanity, courage, and strictness. These are hardly characteristics that would be idealized in today's high-impact, high-action films! These are the character traits of good students—who in turn become great scholars.

It follows that if one is quietly reflective, studious, and insightful, then one must be flexible. Flexibility is critical because, as Sun Tzu states, ". . . *as water has no constant form, there are in war no constant conditions.*" He later says that, "*Of the five elements, none is always predominant; of the four seasons, none is permanent; of the days, some are long and some are short, and the moon waxes and wanes.*"

If there is a "core principle" to understanding Sun Tzu and applying his insights in life and business, it is an attitude of quiet watchfulness and flexibility. It is a Zen "mindfulness" that calls forth seemingly contradictory postures: intense focus while maintaining a fully alert watchfulness. I say seemingly contradictory, because they are anything but contradictory. Intense focus and alert watchfulness are, in fact, mutually sustaining.

Read Sun Tzu again, this time looking for the stance of docility as defined above. You will see it woven throughout his work. Time and again, Sun Tzu admonishes the general to watch, to consider, to weigh, to examine, to listen, to discern. Then, and only then, may one act. Only then, will the actions and tasks of war, or business, be grounded in knowledge, not wishful thinking; and certainly not in hurried, rash aggression.

Most of my colleagues are devotees of management guru Tom Peters, who is not my cup of tea. Peters insists that one achieves success through a "Ready-Fire-Aim" approach to taking action. Peters is openly hostile to those who prefer more thoughtful, studied, and methodical approaches. A recent target of Peters' is Peter Drucker, who is probably the greatest and most admired business management theorist of our time.

I make no apologies that I am as much as a disciple of Peter Drucker as of Sun Tzu. Drucker, in his great work, *The Effective Executive*, states that "Effective executives do not race."

The Master would agree.

Bibliography

Books

von Clausewitz, Carl. *On War.* Princeton, NJ: Princeton University Press, 1976.

Van Creveld, Martin. *Command in War.* Cambridge, MA: Harvard University Press, 1985.

Cohen, William A. *The Art of the Leader.* Englewood Cliffs, NJ, 1990.

Creech, Bill, General. *The Five Pillars of TQM.* New York: Plume/Penguin, 1994.

Dixon, Norman. *On the Psychology of Military Incompetence.* London: Johnathon Cape, 1976.

du Picq, Ardant, Colonel. *Battle Studies.* Harrisburg, PA: The Military Science Publishing Co., 1958.

Fenster, Julie M. *In the Words of Great Business Leaders.* New York: John Wiley & Sons, Inc. 2000.

Fuller, J. F. C. *The Conduct of War.* London: Eyre & Spottiswoode, 1961.

Fulmer, Phillip and Gerald Sentell. *Legacy of Winning.* Out of Print.

Halberstam, David. *The Reckoning.* New York: William Morrow & Company, 1986.

Hart, B. H. Liddel. *Strategy.* New York: Praeger Publishers, 1967.

Henderson, G. F. R., Colonel. *The Science of War.* London: Longmans, Green and Co., 1905.

Johnstone, Henry Melville, Captain. *The Foundations of Strategy.* London: George, Allen & Unwin, 1914.

Levinson, Harry. *The Exceptional Executive.* New York: New American Library, 1971.

Luttwak, Edward N. *On the Meaning of Victory.* New York: Simon and Schuster, 1986.

_____, *The Pentagon and the Art of War.* New York: Simon and Schuster, 1984.

Luttwak, Edward N. and Daniel Horowitz. *The Israeli Army.* Cambridge, MA: Abt Books, 1983.

Michaelson, Gerald A. *Building Bridges to Customers.* Portland, OR: Productivity Press, 1995.

Michaelson, Gerald A. *Winning the Marketing War.* Knoxville, TN: Pressmark International, 1987.

Michaelson, Gerald A. *50 Ways to Close a Sale.* New York: William Morrow and Company, Inc., 1994.

Mahan, A. T. *The Influence of Sea Power upon History.* New York: Hill and Wang, 1957.

Phillips, Thomas R., Major (ed.). *Roots of Strategy.* Westport, CT: Greenwood Press, 1982.

Tye, Joe. *Personal Best.* New York: MIF Books, 1997.

Magazines

Modern Maturity, (AARP), Washington, D.C., Jan.-Feb. 2002.

Newsweek, (Newsweek, Inc.), 444 Madison Avenue, New York, NY 10022, Dec. 17, 2001.

Time, (Time, Inc.), Time & Life Building, Rockefeller Center, New York, NY 10020, Aug. 14, 2001.

Other

Presentation by Benjamin Netanyahu, Detroit, MI, Jan. 5, 2002.

Bibliography
of Translators

Includes only books containing a complete translation.

Ames, Roger. *Sun Tzu: The Art of Warfare*. New York: Ballantine Books, 1993. pp. 321, HB $25.00. Includes analysis, complete text, and "five hitherto unknown chapters."

Bruya, Brian. *Sun Zi Speaks*. [Sun Zi is the Chinese spelling and more clipped phonic of Sun Tzu] New York: Anchor Books, 1966. pp. 139, Paper $10.95. This book is illustrated by Tsai Chih Chung with cartoon-like drawings accompanying each sentence.

Chien-sein Ko. *The Art of War by Sun Tzu in Chinese and English*. Publisher unknown, 1973. Out of print.

Clavell, James. *The Art of War Sun Tzu*. New York: Delta by Dell, 1988. pp. 82, Paper $10.95. Written by a novelist with his interpretations of the ideograms which lack the combative interpretations of military authors.

Cleary, Thomas. *The Art of War Sun Tzu*. Boston & London: Shamballa, 1988. pp. 171, Paper $11.00. Original translation plus extensive commentary by eleven interpreters.

Griffith, Samuel B. *Sun Tzu The Art of War*. London, Oxford, New York: Oxford Press, 1963. pp. 197, Paper $8.95. Also in Hardback. Extensive commentary throughout.

Giles, Lionel. *Sun Tzu on the Art of War*. Publisher unknown, out of print. Includes extensive annotations for every sentence.

Krause, Donald G. *The Art of War for Executives*. New York, Berkley, 1995. pp. 116, Paper $12.00. Lots of interpretive commentary, but may not include entire translation.

Phillips, Major Thomas R. Numerous translations including *The Art of War*. Westport, Connecticut: Greenwood Press, 1940. Hardback and paperback where available.

Sadler, Al. *Three Military Classic of China* (Including Sun Tzu). Sydney: Australasian Medical, 1944. Probably out of print.

Sawyer, Ralph D. *Sun Tzu Art of War*. Boulder, Colorado: Westview Press, 1994. pp. 375, Paper $12.95. Original text plus extensive commentary. *The Complete Art of War Sun Tzu, Sun Pin*. Published in 1996 in Hardback $25.00.

Tang Zi-Chang. *Principles of Conflict*. T. C. Press. Out of print.

Wing, R. L. *The Art of Strategy*. Publisher unknown.

Zang Humin. *Sun Tzu, The Art of War*. Publisher unknown. pp. 327. $14.95. Includes extensive text in Oriental languages and succinct commentary.

Index

Also available by Gerald Michaelson . . .

Sun Tzu: The Art of War for Managers

"Business is war. Michaelson's update of this time-tested classic is required reading for managers who want to prevail."
—Steve Sion, Editor in Chief, *Success* magazine

This new translation of the timeless classic *The Art of War* was discovered by Michaelson while lecturing in China. This business interpretation applies Sun Tzu's wisdom to today's competitive environment. The brilliant insights and invaluable perspectives will help you prevail in every business situation you will encounter.

Learn to:
- Properly assess competitive situations
- Develop strategies that go beyond conventional rules
- Prepare a good defense
- Succeed as a leader
- Move swiftly to disrupt your opponent
- Gather crucial information that gives you a competitive advantage

It also provides specific examples of the applications of Sun Tzu's ideas from successful companies—helping you to understand how you can apply these tactics. Take the strategies from *Sun Tzu: The Art of War for Managers* and win your business battles.

Trade Paperback, $10.95
6" x 9", 224 pages
ISBN: 1-58062-459-6